TRANSSEXUALITY IN THE MALE

Publication Number 1030
AMERICAN LECTURE SERIES®

A Monograph in

The BANNERSTONE DIVISION *of*
AMERICAN LECTURES IN BEHAVIORAL SCIENCE AND LAW

Edited by

RALPH SLOVENKO, B.E., LL.B., M.A., Ph.D.
Wayne State University
Law School
Detroit, Michigan

TRANSSEXUALITY IN THE MALE

The Spectrum of Gender Dysphoria

By

ERWIN K. KORANYI, M.D.
Professor of Psychiatry
University of Ottawa
Royal Ottawa Hospital
Ottawa, Ontario, Canada

With a Foreword by

Ralph Slovenko, B.E., LL.B., M.A., Ph.D.
Wayne State University
Law School
Detroit, Michigan

CHARLES C THOMAS · PUBLISHER
Springfield · Illinois · U.S.A.

Published and Distributed Throughout the World by
CHARLES C THOMAS • PUBLISHER
Bannerstone House
301-327 East Lawrence Avenue, Springfield, Illinois, U.S.A.

© 1980, by CHARLES C THOMAS • PUBLISHER
ISBN 0-398-03924-0
Library of Congress Catalog Card Number: 79-14638

With THOMAS BOOKS *careful attention is given to all details of
manufacturing and design. It is the Publisher's desire to present books
that are satisfactory as to their physical qualities and artistic possibilities
and appropriate for their particular use.* THOMAS BOOKS *will be true
to those laws of quality that assure a good name and good will.*

Library of Congress Cataloging in Publication Data

Koranyi, Erwin K
    Transsexuality in the male.

    (American lecture series; no. 1030)
    Bibliography: p.
    Includes index.
    1. Change of sex. 2. Transvestism. 3. Homosexuality.
4. Men—Sexual behavior. 5. Change of sex—Law and
legislation. I. Title.
RC560.C4K67   616.8'583   79-14638
ISBN 0-398-03924-0

Printed in the United States of America
W-2

To my wife, Edie
my family, friends and patients

CONTRIBUTORS

of Chapters 6 and 7.

NORMAN B. BARWIN, M.D., Associate Professor of Obstetrics and Gynecology, University of Ottawa, Ottawa General Hospital, Ottawa, Ontario, Canada.

BETTY J. LYNCH, M.Ps., Psychologist, Department of Forensic Psychiatry, Royal Ottawa Hospital, Ottawa, Ontario, Canada.

SELWYN M. SMITH, M.D., Associate Professor of Psychiatry, University of Ottawa, Royal Ottawa Hospital, Ottawa, Ontario, Canada.

FOREWORD

Sex, a favorite subject since the beginning of time, has only recently come under scientific scrutiny. The study of sex as a separate scientific endeavor began in the nineteenth century, with biologists focusing on reproduction and psychiatrists focusing on sexual aberrations. This book by Dr. Erwin K. Koranyi is a contribution to the investigation of transsexuality, transvestism and homosexuality in the male.

The target of Dr. Koranyi's study is transsexuality, with transvestism and homosexuality discussed mainly as they relate to transsexuality. Transsexuality is considered a distinct entity but with a still unclear etiology. Dr. Koranyi points out that the first symptoms of this condition are sometimes manifested at an amazingly young age. Age one year, he finds, is the earliest for gender identity disturbance, and age two is quite frequent. Cases with later manifestations are also observed. Thus, there is need for a careful evaluation of both the biological and the psychological factors.

Pure clinical manifestation of transsexualism is not always the case, and an overlap between transsexualism and some form of transvestism or homosexuality frequently occurs. The unique features of transsexualism are the consuming urge to crossdress, the single-minded determination to become a member of the opposite anatomical sex and an intense dislike of one's own anatomical sex, sometimes existing to the point of self-castration. Suicide is a frequent occurrence among transsexuals. Dr. Koranyi observes that psychotherapy does not represent a viable means for treating these disorders. He suggests, however, that a good psychosocial adaptation can be achieved in carefully selected cases with surgical and sex hormone therapies. The careful selection and evaluation of the suitable cases are the task of gender identity clinics where a team of professionals assesses each patient individually. Transsexualism and transsexual surgery is no longer an esoteric phenomenon, and there are now thousands of people who have undergone such procedures. Transsexual surgery became a reality when a GI named George (now Christine) Jorgensen underwent a sex change operation in 1952 in Denmark, astounding the world.

Since the biological and the psychological roots of sexuality are intermeshed, both of these factors need to be assessed appropriately. The overlap between maleness and femaleness is considerable both from the biological and psychological dimension. Dr. Koranyi points out that the sexual partner choice in some instances leads back to a single hormone injection given to the mother for medical reasons during the sensitive stages of her pregnancy. Thus, what was believed to be a "free choice," influenced only by psychosocial and environmental factors, turns out in the individual's life many years later to be a biologically determined event. To be sure, this does not mean that psychological and adaptational circumstances can be ignored during the formative years of an individual, as they are capable of reinforcing or ameliorating a biologically rooted factor.

Developments in medicine and science continually challenge the legal system. The legal profession must take cognizance of these developments and their impact upon society. Transsexual surgery (the technical steps of the procedure are ably described by Dr. Norman B. Barwin in a contributing chapter of this book) poses considerable problems to the law. The law is based on certain fundamental assumptions about sex, namely, there are two and only two sexes, male and female. Transsexuality is a dilemma and a controversy not only in medicine and psychiatry but also in law. How is the law to regard the postsurgery transsexual? Renee Richards, the male ophthalmologist-turned-female tennis pro, ignited a storm of controversy about whether chromosomes are to determine tournament eligibility. Should such individuals be legally recognized by the new sex? If such a person has to be sent to jail, should "he" or "she" be sent to a male or female prison? What about a father's will giving his inheritance to his son who in the interim became his "daughter"? Dr. Selwyn M. Smith and Betty J. Lynch in a contributing chapter discuss these and many other questions that are still far from settled.

In undertaking this book, Dr. Koranyi draws upon a background rich in study and experience. Born in 1924 in Budapest, Hungary, and surviving the Nazi Holocaust, he began his medical training in 1945 at the University of Budapest. He left Hungary in 1949 and continued his medical studies and obtained his medical degree in 1950 at the University of Innsbruck, Austria. He had his internship in West Germany and then worked as a general practitioner in Israel, undertaking a position as the first physician in the city of Eilath. He subsequently did neurophysiological research at the Max Planck Institute in Cologne, Germany. In late 1952 he immigrated to Canada and began work as a resident in psychiatry at the Verdum Protestant Hospital.

Dr. Koranyi is now Head of the Neuropsychiatric Investigation Unit and Director of Educaton at the Royal Ottawa Hospital. He was named Professor in Psychiatry in 1975 at the University of Ottawa. He is a member of a number of professional associations and the author of over thirty major articles in scientific journals. He was awarded the Israeli War Ribbon for services in the Yom Kippur War, was elected "Best Clinical Professor of the Year 1977" by Student Council of the Faculty of Medicine, University of Ottawa, and was elected Honorary Class President by the Medical Students of 1978, Faculty of Medicine, University of Ottawa.

RALPH SLOVENKO
Editor

ACKNOWLEDGMENTS

THE PURPOSE OF this monograph is to highlight some of the controversial medical and legal issues pertinent to the subject of transsexualism in particular, as it relates to transvestism and homosexuality in the male. The clinical delineation of these conditions, the complexity of their overlap, the as yet unclear etiologies are described here. I have attempted to navigate my language between the Scylla and Charybdis of the medical and legal terminologies.

I wish to express my gratitude to Ralph Slovenko, Professor of Law and Psychiatry, Wayne State University, Detroit, Michigan, for the fact that this monograph was written at his personal instigation and encouragement, and also because he kindly consented to write an introduction. Recognition is expressed here to G. J. Sarwer-Foner, M.D., Professor and Chairman, Department of Psychiatry, Faculty of Medicine in the University of Ottawa, for his participation and contribution to our Gender Identity Clinic.

I wish to acknowledge the efforts of Dr. Selwyn M. Smith and Betty J. Lynch and Dr. Norman Barwin for having contributed two valuable chapters. I wish to thank Mrs. Pat Butter for her helpful editorial suggestions and the Department of Communications of the University of Ottawa for providing the professional illustrations. I am also obliged to the helpful staff of Charles C Thomas, Publisher.

A special gratitude is expressed to my secretary, Mrs. Mary Ann Dugal, for her devotion, patience and endurance. I also wish to thank my dear wife, Edie, for her loving kindness and for having put up with the lost evenings and weekends and the constant turmoil in the den.

Erwin K. Koranyi

CONTENTS

TRANSSEXUALITY IN THE MALE

CHAPTER 1

SPECTRUM OF SOME SEXUAL DISORDERS

INTRODUCTORY REMARKS ON SEXUALITY

Rapid accumulation of new data and evolvement of recent views concerning the scientific, behavioral, social and legal dimensions of human sexuality demand frequent monographic review. The present publication is intended to be a collection of diversified knowledge of some of the unconventional forms of male sexual practices. A discussion of female sexuality was excluded from this work because of the relative paucity of first-hand clinical material available to this author.

The exclusive focus on the social and global behavioral aspects of sexuality and the corresponding neglect of the biological influence has contributed to a pervasive and tenacious public opinion based on generalizations, simplifications and misconceptions. Since clinical sexual problems in each instance represent individual, and proportionately significant, composites of biological, psychological and social factors, it is mandatory that basic concepts of all three factors be provided as a prerequisite for the understanding of deviant sexuality. Monographs attempting to describe and integrate every parameter, including biological aspects, of this subject, are often less popular.

Impelled by the eagerness for an immediate grasp of the central theme, one might easily lose sight of the need to understand the basic elements of normal sexuality, with its biological, psychosocial and cultural ramifications, as a prerequisite in comprehending deviant sexuality.

A problematic issue is the finding of a suitable language and an appropriate depth in order to accommodate the readers' varied needs and interests. Some of the elaborations must, of necessity, be technical and detailed and therefore seemingly

3

remote to some readers. This difficulty, however, will be eased by means of interspersed explanations, popular language, a minimum of references to the extensive literature and a glossary of technical terms.

Most scientific writings begin with an assembly of definitions, which ultimately fall victim to further elaborations, exceptions and qualifications. This monograph is no exception. The subjects must be defined; yet a spectrum, by its very meaning, can offer no sharp demarcation.

Disordered sexuality, properly defined, logically necessitates the establishment of the form and the range of sexual normalcy. "Normal" in a biological and behavioral realm is a mere statistical approximation rather than an ethical-moral issue. For the sake of convenience, it is more appropriate to talk about a range of normal sexuality, not unlike a reference to any other normal range of biological data, such as the pulse rate or blood sugar level. This is not to be misunderstood, by a perversion of logic, as a promulgation of the notion that the absence of a sharp delineation of the normal patently eliminates the concept of the abnormal. For example, no matter how persistently one inquires about such trivial data as the normal value of blood pressure, instead of a range of rigid figures one encounters ifs, buts and ambiguities relating to the relative role of many variables. Yet no one would deny the very real existence of the pathological state of hypertension. Thus, the elusiveness of the concept of "normal" is not peculiar singularly to behavioral sciences but happens to be equally prevalent in medicine and in biology. A special emphasis is placed on this particular point because of the recent "antipsychiatric movement," promoted by Thomas Szasz, R. D. Laing, O. Hobart Mowrer and others. Through a dislocation of reasoning, they have arrived at the absurd conclusion that the vagueness in defining normalcy automatically liquidates the concept of abnormal and thus have stated that the existence of mental illness is a myth.

Anthropologists and transculturalists are limited to the comparative description of the different social values, life-styles and habits of separate cultures. The causes of these adaptive variables in different cultures are complex and frequently inscrutable. Nevertheless, the divergence in social values, including those referring to sexual behavior, is enormous. This divergence is illustrated by the fact that a particular sexual act in our day and age might be dealt with by the public beheading of the "culprits" in one society, while in another culture the same act might occur frequently and be regarded as one's own private business.

Even within the same society sharp differences will prevail. Different moral standards are applied to, or expected of, the male and the female, the young and the old, the rich and the poor, or the fair and the unattractive. Acts, of course, are also judged according to the setting in which they occur. Stereotypic imagery and purely mental elaboration will radically alter the male response to a woman dressed in bra and panties versus a woman in a bikini swimsuit, even if the garments are all of the same material, color and cut.

History, which usually offers insight, extends little help in the effort to locate a baseline for the normal. Instead, its rich material blurs the issue even further. The strikingly discordant and extremely undulating mores from one historical period to the next are well known. The sexual permissiveness typical of a particular era and location alternates unpredictably with the extreme rigor and narrowmindedness of another. In the same period of history when the "abominable crime of buggery" was incorporated into the written law, and when Queen Victoria, in her total disbelief as to its existence, refused to legislate against lesbianism, the world of Fanny Hill prevailed and Toulouse-Lautrec's cheerful bordellos enjoyed a happy existence. Unofficially, however, the real crime was considered to be not the inherent "immorality" of a certain sexual act itself but the sad event of being caught—a principle having had an admirable survival capacity throughout the ages. Such was the case with an unfortunate hen that, mistakenly thought to be a rooster, was publicly executed in Basel in 1474 by the authorities of the Church, along with the three eggs "he" laid (*Ciba-Zeitschrift*, 1952). Similarly, twenty people and two dogs were executed for lechery in Salem, Massachusetts, in 1692 (Evans, 1971).

The law, the community and people in general judge others by their actual or suspected behavior. Except for religious confessions and some poetry, little was known of the diversity of human sexual fantasy until the advent of psychoanalysis. Yet judgment and self-control, fragile and sometimes easily eroded modalities of the mind, lie between the act and the fantasy. From society's viewpoint, the judging of individuals by their actual behavior, rather than by their fantasies, might be correct and practical. However, fantasy, frequently the precursor of behavior, is evidently valued differently by psychiatrists. Without ever putting their hidden thoughts into actual practice or verbal expression, most people entertain periodic or continual extremes of fantasy in their day or nighttime sexual imagery, a fact well known to those who deal with human behavior. Therein lies the imperishable success of "obscene" literature.

BASIC BIOLOGICAL AND PSYCHOLOGICAL ASPECTS OF SEXUALITY

Studies of hermaphroditism, the condition of ambiguous or abnormal human and animal genital organs, have captured the interest of physicians and naturalists since ancient times. Both Anaxagoras (c. 500-428 B.C.) and Hippocrates (c. 460-377 B.C.) contributed to the subject, and the concern with its understanding has never ceased throughout the ages. In spite of even earlier knowledge of the considerably more common homosexuality, hermaphroditism was not seriously studied scientifically until 1886. The first clinical treastise, *Psychopathia Sexualis*, by Richard von Krafft-Ebing, president of the then influential Viennese Neurological Society, heralded the beginning of serious interest in the problem of sexual deviations. The impact of these engendered scientific investigations came in the early 1920s through the work of Magnus Hirschfeld, Sigmund Freud, G. C. Jung, Alfred Adler, Otto Weininger and Havelock Ellis. Apart from the question of overt homosexuality itself, the emerging issue was the gradual recognition of those principles that were widely applicable to the grasp of the universal sexual development. An original matrix of potential human bisexuality was assumed to be prevalent and represented in everyone, at least in a rudimentary form. This concept was expressed by Freud's hypothesis of the "polymorphous perverse" nature of the human infant; by Jung's assumption of coexisting male and female parts (animus, anima), with either dominant, in everyone; and by Adler's theory of universal "psychic hermaphroditism." Thus, maleness and femaleness were no longer viewed as diametrically opposite and mutually exclusive situations of "either/or" character but as an admixture of both with the prevalence of features of one or the other.

Scientific hypotheses arise from assumptions and are the subjects of pending disputes, verifications, modifications or rejection. Sometimes these hypotheses are retained to serve as convenient models for the understanding of a function until they are replaced by something better. Regardless of which contingents of Freud's theories might eventually survive the test of time, some of his observations concerning infant sexuality have contributed significantly to the current insight into adult sexuality. Noted is the fact that Freud, himself Victorian and rather prudish, was thoroughly shocked when he first encountered the wide variety of sexual fantasies verbalized by his earliest patients. In order to obtain the flow of these thoughts, he utilized a method of free association first described by Galton and modified by himself and Jung. The fantasies presented included rape, incest, masochism, sadism and homosexuality. Having eventually been able to view the expressions of his patients with a scientific detachment and having studied his own fantasies, Freud traced the roots of such imagery to the evolving sexuality of the infant. Increasingly, he discerned the nucleus of a pleasure-seeking human-animal fragment of the mind, motivated by a relentless raw drive, or instinct, seeking satisfaction. This aspect of the mind—the Id—was described by Freud as being "polymorphous perverse" (an awkward term lending itself to misinterpretation), inasmuch as it concerned itself exclusively with total and immediate gratification regardless of its source and nature. From 1938 on, neurophysiologists such as Papez, MacLean and others came to identify a particular brain area, the limbic system, as largely related to such behavioral functions. Other modalities of the mind having to do with the appreciation of reality (Ego) and the evolvement of the conscience (Superego), which permitted eventually integrated social functioning, were still to be developed in the infant when the Id was already present as an operant entity.

An important tenet in Freud's outlined construct of mind function was his assertion that the primitive pleasure-seeking component, the Id, bound to brain tissue as far as its ongoing striving is concerned, never dissolves, disappears or mingles with other, later-developed modalities of the apparatus. Instead, it retains its original character forever and continues to coexist as an independent partner, partly determining behavior. To be sure, in its raw form, the Id is superseded or "outvoted" by other, acquired modalites related to higher social developments, the latter imposing suppression, postponement and modifications upon the unwilling primitive urges in order to attain socially acceptable and adaptive conduct. The "dark forces" of the Id, nonetheless, are perpetually looming in the background. Testifying to the existence of these concealed drives is the behavioral observation of brain-damaged adults in whom the highest critical and judgmental modalities, peeled off as a result of the damage, no longer screen out the original primitive strivings, which become once again exposed and unrestrained.

A logical sequence of the aforementioned propositions is the fact that every human contains a certain share of sexual vagueness, in not only the psychological but also the biological realm. For example, both the male and the female produce testosterone and estrogen. Rudimentary female organs—the breasts—begin to grow in the male in certain physical conditions, and facial hair growth is a problem in some postmenopausal females. Nevertheless, determination of sexual identity, a task usually done successfully by most laymen without special qualifications, can at times represent a considerable medical problem. This is why the term *sex* must be broken down into a variety of subcategories:

Chromosomal sex
Nuclear sex
Hormonal sex
Gonadal sex
    external genitalia
    internal genitalia
Gender sex
    core gender identity
    sexual role, gender behavior

A detailed discussion pertaining to these overlapping modalities will be supplied in the subsequent chapters. A brief outline at this point, however, will help to clarify these concepts.

Chromosomal sex, determined at the moment of conception, refers to a person's typically male (46XY) or typically female (46XX) constellation of chromosomes, present in each cell. It is to be noted that there are many exceptions to the rule and that the sex chromosome abnormality happens to be the most common form of genetic deviance. Not only can crossed-over sex chromosome patterns (XX male and XY female) exist, but numerical excess or insufficiency of X or Y chromosomes frequently can cause varying degrees of pathological consequences. There are cases where both the male XY and the female XX coexist in the tissues of the same individual, resulting in what is known as true hermaphroditism. From a chromosomal point of view, such conditions are referred to as mosaicism, i.e. the simultaneous occurrence of different chromosomal lines operant within the same individual. Translocation is another abnormality whereby the specific genetic role of a particular chromosome was transposed onto another. The most diverse kinds of such translocations have been observed.

Nuclear sex is determined by a test that demonstrates the presence or absence of a dark-staining dot—the sex chromatin, or Barr body—within the cells of a person. The presence of such a structure proves that the individual has at least two X chromosomes and thus, save for some chromosomal abnormality (such as Klinefelter's syndrome), is a female. The presence of such sex chromatin remains unaltered for life; neither hormone treatment nor sex-change surgery influence its existence.

Hormonal sex is determined by the typical male or cyclic female pattern of quantitative hormone production in an individual. Again, exceptions and abnormalities concerning these parameters can be found; for example, individuals with perfect external female appearance, male 46XY chromosomal pattern and high male levels of testosterone excretion (testicular feminization syndrome) may be found.

The presence or absence of hormone-producing tissues determines the gonadal sex. Male and female types of tissues secreting both hormones may coexist simultaneously in a person, usually with a high propensity to develop malignant hormone-producing tumors. Whether male or female, the fetus in the earliest stage is characterized by the presence of a neutral genital tissue called the indifferent gonad, which at this stage possesses inherent capacity to develop into either of the two sexes. Subsequently, promoted by a chemical component present in the short arm of the Y chromosome, testosterone begins to be produced in the fetus, causing the heretofore neutral indifferent gonad to evolve towards its potential male development. The absence or the inefficiency of this testosterone secretion in the fetus at this particular "critical stage" of development, regardless of the male chromosomal pattern, will cause the fetus to evolve along the female line of development, as the "basic" sex happens to be female. This inherent capacity of the fetus to develop potentially into either male or female is referred to as sexual dimorphism. The development of internal and external genitalia is not necessarily parallel, and the two might, in the same individual, evolve in opposite or ambiguous directions. It is of fundamental importance that the genetic, hormonal, drug and environmental factors be capable of bringing about decisive and irreversible influences during the critical stages of intra-uterine development and that they determine an eventual male or female appearance. These factors may even affect future sexual choices and behavior manifested for the first time many years later. Experimental evidence in animals indicates that, beyond the already mentioned factors, diet, pollutants, insecticides and chemicals are capable of dislocating otherwise normal sexual growth and of causing abnormal sexual behavior.

Gender sex is thought to develop after birth and is expressed by a growing recognition of belonging to the male or to the female sex. Thus, the infant acquires a core gender identity—an internal awareness of, and ideally a harmony with, his/her sexual belonging. Environmental constituents, in the form of mothering style, parental expectations and the apparent imposition of contemporary stereotypic sexual roles, are considered to be the major elements in shaping the infant's evolvement. Sexual role and gender behavior emerge under the influence of a series of positive and negative reinforcements by the environment in regard to the child's age- and sex-appropriate behavior. These formative influences, reaching the infant over a period of time, also contain a flow of individual configuration in those satisfactions and frustrations that are encountered by him or her within the fabric of infant-parent relationships and are considered to be the decisive determinants in attaining a gender identity. It should be noted, however, that the influence of the milieu by itself represents a nonspecific force. Many children undergo environmental influences generally considered to be adverse in respect to development of their gender identity without necessarily manifestng sexually deviant behavior later. Others, who grow in a favorable milieu, sometimes do develop sexual disturbances.

The vast majority of infants at this early postnatal stage are physically unambiguous males or females. Biological components playing a role in their future sexuality (to the extent it is present or operant) are probably the most subtle kind and have therefore had insufficient study. It is remarkable that some social psychiatrists, who are prepared to place disproportionate importance upon yet unverified and minuscule environmental events in the early psychosexual milieu of an infant, are often quite indifferent, if not negative, towards the significance of subtle biological factors that are often quite capable of deflecting future sexual development. Notable exceptions are those analysts, such as Stoller (1969), who have dealt with sufficiently large numbers of transsexuals. True and typical transsexualism is thought to develop in a biologically vulnerable individual prompted by very early influences in the milieu. The relative importance of these two determinants varies from one case to another.

According to Money (1969), gender identity is acquired at an amazingly young age, before and around the age of eighteen months. First signs of transsexual development have been described by Stoller (1966-67) and others as occurring around one or two years of age, which is substantially younger than was hitherto assumed by psychoanalysts. Because core gender identity amalgamates at such an early age, Money and co-workers (1969) suggest that sex-altering surgery in anatomically malformed children should be performed before eighteen months of age if technically feasible.

Sexual drive, present since birth (though naturally not expressed in its adult form), is steadily influenced by a multitude of biological and environmental events as it slowly unfolds. In the very early stages of development, the single most important impact is probably represented by the psychobiological process of mothering — a complex and circular transaction between mother and infant. As this most intricate process is a powerful modifier of both the psychological and biological ultimate outcome, it will receive detailed description later in this book.

In comparison to other species, the human infant is born at the least completed stage of development. Simply put, the human infant has already been born and is living an extrauterine life at a point of biological development when the offspring of other species are still protected from the environment and are continuing to grow within the intrauterine world. This is so despite the duration of the human pregnancy, for it is the inherent speed of tissue maturation, not simply the length of pregnancy, that matters. This stage of comparative human underdevelopment at birth accounts for the infant's postnatal vulnerability and determines his/her proclivity for responding to environmental influences in a profound manner. At the same time, this undifferentiated stage "plasticity" is precisely one of the factors permitting the human to achieve higher levels of learning.

Exceedingly helpless and dependent for survival on both mother and milieu, the infant's capacity to perceive the most subtle environmental hints is truly an amazing phenomenon. As growth progresses, the infant's biological matrix and the environmental factors meet, mingle and interact. Step by step, the infant is exposed to increasing parental expectations, expanding role assignment, sexual comparing and contrasting with peers, and contemporary social-cultural demands. Initially faltering, but becoming increasingly bolder, the infant begins to manifest his/her inner- and outer-determined sexual identity and an age-approximate sexual role.

Just as delicate biological development passes through distinct critical phases and pitfalls of development from the moment of conception, so too, psychological growth, from birth on, has its own crucial sequential stages, each loaded with potential hazards. It is important to emphasize, however, that any separation of the biological and psychological processes is entirely artificial. Such arbitrary division is in reality nonexistent since the two modalities continually interact, are interdependent and, in fact, merely represent different approaches to the same system. Oversight of this point might, and often does, lead to scientifically intolerable simplifications, resulting in remote theoretical speculations and a kind of thinking where metaphors and anecdotes are mistaken for scientific data. Professionals employing such thinking were appropriately referred to as "word merchants" by Mandel (1976). Therefore, only the closest consideration of both the biological and psychological factors can bring about any degree of valid understanding.

Early childhood, the early teen years and beyond are universally characterized by sexual experimentation of various natures. Playing "house" or "doctor," with subsequent innocuous heterosexual and homosexual experimentation is ubiquitous. Such isolated events may be meaningless until a series of these events begins to follow a discernible pattern in which the child's assumed roles become more or less fixated or his/her preferences distinct; at this point, the future sexual orientation, reflecting conventional or unconventional features, begins to amalgamate. The repeated satisfaction accompanying a particular preference will create an increasing need for more of the same kind, thus providing accumulated experiences, reinforcements and habituation.

The universally present nucleus for biological and psychological bisexual potential has already been mentioned, as has been the original inherent sexual interest in both conventional and unconventional modalities, prevalent in all. The ultimate coagulation of a highly individual repertoire of sexual expression depends on a multitude of somatic factors and on environmental contributors, the two being inseparably intertwined.

The understanding of the hierarchical nature of brain development is of remarkable clinical and even medico-legal significance. As the brain matures both neurologically and psychologically in its sequential stages, the individual functions mainly at the highest layer of hierarchy attained. Of crucial importance is the fact that none of the earlier developmental layers is ever abolished; remaining stored, they are merely surpassed and dominated by the new and higher order of addition. Thus, the layer-upon-layer style of the arrangement of the neuropsychiatric system is comparable to an onion, which, in its intact form, reveals only its outer surface. In the case of a neuropsychiatric disturbance, however, the highest hierarchical layer partially or totally peels off, relinquishing the leadership to less integrated and cruder developmental stages until they are suppressed. Depending on the nature of the disturbance, such a state can be either temporary or permanent. Damage affecting mostly the neurological modalities of the brain will result in so-called pathologic reflexes—reflexes that in infancy were normal but that, reappearing in the adult, signify a distinct pathology. Similarly, transient or permanent brain impairment in the behavioral realm will result in indiscriminate sexual, aggressive or other forms of primitive behavior or regression.

SEX: CONVENTIONAL AND UNCONVENTIONAL

Sexual activity in the animal world is known to be an unvaried, unitary and stereotypic act with little variation as to the manner in which it is performed, comparable almost to a reflex action. Human sexuality is variable not only from one individual to the next but, to a degree, from one act to another. What, then, are the determinants responsible for the manifestation of a particular ultimate sexual style? Let us answer these questions with more questions: What is the final constellation of preferences that will emerge from the lottery of dormant potentials? What is the relative importance or amount of compelling force behind each of these components? What is the sum total of an individual's sexual drive? What past memories and reinforcements represent unknown quanta of urges? In what kaleidoscopic manner does sexual style tally or collide with the rest of the personality and with the social-cultural milieu of the individual? In what fashion does an individual's total physical makeup facilitate, inhibit or cancel out his/her interests? How compatible is an individual's particular sexual style with the needs and expectations of his/her partner? Not unlike an artist's palette with its few basic colors yielding endless shades, the final result of a person's sexual style is greatly determined by the answers to these numerous questions.

Readily recognized is the fact that we are all voyeurs but that the male in particular is prone to it and that "girl watching" is a favorite activity for many. This fact is duly reflected in the nature of television commercials. The issue is the particular manner in which it is practised: a pleasing glance, an ogling stare, a deliberate positioning, or climbing a ladder in an alley at night to peek into someone's bathroom. Its full and extreme form is referred to as perversion. While on a small scale men tend to be voyeurs, in a complementary fashion and, equally harmlessly, women show mild degrees of exhibitionism.

Similarly, and almost exclusively, the male tends to be a fetishist; he finds intimate female garments and "forbidden" objects sexually arousing, presumably because at an early age he admired such articles on an alluring female and also because they enhanced his image of femaleness. His desire to have the sexual partner occasionally wear such items during the sexual act in order to enhance arousal is quite common. When it is an exclusive condition for sexual readiness, the harmless act then becomes dominant. A full-fledged fetishist excludes the sexual partner altogether and uses the garment or article by itself for solitary sexual pleasure. Fetishists will sometimes steal such garments, usually from the laundry line, not only because they are too shy to purchase such articles in a store but also because they might require the added pleasure of knowing that the particular item has actually been worn by a female. Thus, for them such an act becomes anonym sex "by proxy." Some prostitutes profit from selling their worn panties to such interested customers.

Sadism and masochism are emotive ingredients with a sexual tinge. It is said that the male exhibits a higher propensity to the former modality and the female to the latter, although reversed distributions are quite common. The two, being linked, are usually referred to as sadomasochism.

On a minor scale and with the consent of the parties involved, sadomasochism can be regarded as a harmless variant of no consequence if pleasurable to both and injurious to neither.

Once it is a dominant factor or an exclusive condition for sexual pleasure, it becomes an increasing problem. If sadistic or masochistic practices assume a serious rather than symbolic form and inflict injury—with or without the consent of either party—they are within the realm of the perversions. It is of utmost importance to remember that many women have periodic or frequent rape fantasies. However, such harmless fantasies have absolutely nothing to do with actual rape, nor do they in any way represent an invitation for rape. The same woman who in privacy may entertain playful daydreams of being raped or may enjoy harmless solitary sex while thinking of being "taken" or being "possessed by a strong man" would in fact be horrified if rape actually became a reality. Often these distinctions are not clearly understood by legal authorities.

In all of these instances is evident a gradated transition from the universal and harmless forms of indulgence to the extreme and distinctly deviant sort.

Childhood and early teens are periods during which frank sexual experiences occur or experiences take place that subsequently become sexualized. Memories of such events are capable of forming tenacious imprints, imprints that may never abate and that have a stubborn tendency to form a compelling urge for their repetition with modifications or their acting out in later life. Depending on its nature and on the frequency of the urge for repetition, such an imprint occasionally might find an outlet between married couples. Often, however, it is used as a masturbational fantasy because of shame or guilt about its unusual character, or it is practised with prostitutes, many of whom are known to be "specialized" in certain roles (Fig. 1-1).

THE WEAKER SEX

Biologists and physicians are aware that the male is the weaker sex. The female, with her XX sex chromosome composition, possesses more chromosome material than the XY male. This difference is offset by a genetic process called dosage compensation, although some geneticists argue that the equalization process is not entirely complete and that the male ultimately remains with 3 to 5 percent less genetic material than the female.

Larger in body than the female, with a higher brain weight

(the latter having no bearing on the IQ), the male has a considerably lower life expectancy. Violence, accident and suicide rates, possibly related to testosterone levels, are also higher in the male. From childhood on, infectious diseases occur more frequently in the male and carry a more serious prognosis. Warren J. Gadpaille (1972) in a brilliant paper, pointed out the higher biological and sexual vulnerability of the male.

Sexual development is more complex, and biological interference more frequent, in the male fetus. In the case of developmental failure in the fetal stage, nature falls back on the underlying female line of development, as biologically the female is the basic sex.

Adult male sexuality is also more prone to disturbances than is that of the female. An absolute prerequisite to the act of coitus is an erection. Erection in the male is not volitional and is most easily interfered with by biological and psychological factors, unlike voluntary female submission to the sexual act, even in the absence of her sexual readiness. An attempt at "trying to force it" only makes matters worse. Emotional and social expectations placed on the sexual success of the male create a popular and frequent, though unjust, way of equating it with other desirable intellectual or leadership qualities. Thus, unreasonable self-expectations can sometimes undermine his sexual confidence. A single sexual failure amounts to somewhat of a disaster and leaves him with a feeling of unease for his next sexual encounter. Impotence in a young man may prevent his marrying, while in later life it may interfere with his marital happiness. The female equivalent of impotence—frigidity—represents a hindrance neither to marriage nor to motherhood, nor does it necessarily abrogate the sexual happiness of her partner.

In sexually malformed children with ambiguous sex organs, the decision in surgical sex reassignment is frequently in favor of the female sex.

The male's need for more esoteric sexual stimuli, visual arousal and indulgence in "obscene" literature is greater than that of the female. Almost all sexual deviations occur more frequently in the male.

TRANSVESTISM

The fetishist either admires female clothing worn by a female sexual partner or, in a more advanced form, becomes enamored with the inanimate item itself. At that stage, he no longer requires the physical presence of an actual sexual partner, his fantasies being sufficient to provide him with his seclusive pleasure. The transvestite, however, actually wears these enticing objects. Therein lies the meager difference between the fetishist and the transvestite.

Transvestism need not, and as a rule does not, involve the act of complete crossdressing. A single item of preferred lingerie, such as a pair of panties or stockings, is sufficient for his purpose of attaining immediate sexual arousal. The desired garments are often excessively "sexy" and more frequently of the kind portrayed in the sexually explicit magazines than those actually worn by women in their everyday lives. Typically, the purpose of the act is the achievement of sexual excitement. The transvestite longs for the physical sensation awakened in him by the touch of such attire and his liberty to "explore" what this nylon clothing hides, even though that is the little-cared-for reality of his own male body. What matters to him is the particular way in which his fantasies alter the real situation. The repetition of the act ending in orgasm reinforces the entity of the experience.

Men, usually in their teens, who are too shy to actually approach the fervently desired female, are especially prone to "trying out" such an experience and may eventually be captured by the practice. What the man dares not do to a female, he does to himself. Once habituated, the urge attains an autonomy of its own and dominates his life from there on. He might, but rarely, retain this outlet on an exclusive basis. More frequently, an additional, parallel and more conventional sex life develops that permits him to marry, father children and sustain a male life-style. He succumbs only periodically to his secret and usually guilt-ridden addiction, either alone or in the company of specialized prostitutes. In rare instances, an understanding wife, wishing to be helpful, will allow such indulgences on the part of her husband, but all too often this is with reluctance and leads to an eventual erosion of her respect and love for him.

This description illustrates the fact that the real transvestite is usually not a homosexual. Far from it. He adores females; he is a veritable secret admirer of women, and his fondest wish would be to live his life in a world filled exclusively with women. Degrees of masochism are often accompanying features of transvestism. His partial, or sometimes complete, crossdressing, accompanied by his sexual arousal, expresses an intense desire to be so close to women that he momentarily pretends to be one. An early childhood history of extreme mother-to-sister closeness, from which he felt excluded, is frequently a traceable element. (Fig. 1-1.)

The transvestite does not wish to get rid of his penis; he merely wishes to hide it. After having reached sexual satisfaction, he reverts to being a man and, with guilt and disgust, quickly removes or even discards the female garb. He then lives his male role until the next temptation emerges. This also explains the fact that the majority of transvestites do not aspire to a credibly feminine appearance. The first transvestite the author saw as a medical student in the Neuropsychiatric Institute in Budapest was a sturdy, married coal miner who had six children and a burly black beard.

Transvestites, however, vary individually. Some are fascinated by lesbians and may even live with them. For some, the credibly feminine appearance does eventually become an overriding issue. Others wish to extend their crossdressing throughout their available free time and over weekends. Displaying their desire to live among women, transvestites join various "sisterhoods" of male-feminism and for private purposes assume part-time female names. At this stage the sexual arousal produced by the act of crossdressing might slowly abate. They do, nevertheless, readily attribute the sensuous feelings they experience in crossdressing to actual women and persuade themselves that the act of ordinary everyday dressing represents an erotic act to all females. Such fantasies are sometimes expressed in letters or articles written by them to certain magazines, describing in minute detail the "pleasure" of dressing, which, of course, is incomprehensible nonsense to an actual woman. These literary pieces are invariably signed with assumed female names.

Some transvestites, being veritable perfectionists, strive for an indistinguishable feminine appearance, the ultimate proof of which is the seduction of a man. In this way, the transvestite occasionally, but usually unsatisfactorily, involves himself in a homosexual act. Having an adaptable sexual potential, some eventually become bisexuals or homosexuals and might even convince themselves to get rid of their sexual organ via surgery, which, if performed, might lead to regret or worse.

A vivid description of teenage transvestism is well portrayed in the case of one of the author's patients. As a young boy in his early teens, filled with sexual craving for girls, he had frequent fantasies and temptations "to slide his hand up the skirt of a girl." His timidity and sexual guilt feelings prevented him from attempting such a thing. One day, at home alone, he spotted his sister's party dress on her bed. He, "for some reason," held the dress in front of himself and saw in the mirror a "skirt and a pair of legs." Finally, he had the opportunity to do what he so craved. He put the dress on and, without fear of rejection or adverse consequences, performed the long-desired act, which proved to be of an imprinting nature. From then on the urge to repeat the act became a constant desire and also altered his life. Eventually he became a female impersonator, though not a homosexual.

The frequency of fetishism-transvestism in the population remains an unaccounted figure, without even reliable estimates. The constant presence of advertisements offering oversized female lingerie in sex magazines sold mainly to men may provide a hint as to the frequency of fetishistic or transvestite practices.

MALE HOMOSEXUALITY

Volumes of books, miles of movie films and television programs, a profusion of symposia and a multitude of scientific and popular publications concerning the nature, presumed causes and social issues of homosexuality have reached large segments, but by no means all, of the public. It would be both presumptuous and futile on the part of the author to provide even a modest summary in a single chapter on this complex issue. Therefore, this brief discussion will be restricted to those selected features that are necessary for a basic understanding of homosexuality as it relates to transvestism and transsexuality. In a salient fashion, some other features of homosexuality will be reiterated.

Homosexuality is a universal phenomenon that has existed in all historical ages, places and cultures. It is not an exclusive human behavior, for it exists in many species of animals with a species-specific rate of frequency, regardless of whether or not the animal lives in captivity or in the natural habitat with equal access to the opposite sex.

Long stigmatized as a sin, crime or sickness, only in 1964 was it first proposed by the Wolfenden report in England that homosexuality between consenting adults be decriminalized. Although the Parliamentary motion was initially defeated, the report itself signalled a turning point concerning the issue of homosexuality in the Western world. In 1974, the American Psychiatric Association, by majority vote, deleted homosexuality from the official list of diseases.

In spite of the common knowledge of homosexuality, its more concise definition remains a puzzling issue. Kinsey, in his famous survey of male (1948) and female (1953) sexuality, examined the incidence of homosexuality and set up a seven-point scale for evaluating sexual behavior:

0—exclusively heterosexual
1—largely heterosexual but with incidental homosexual history
2—largely heterosexual but with distinct homosexual history
3—equally heterosexual and homosexual
4—largely homosexual but with distinct heterosexual history
5—largely homosexual but with incidental heterosexual history
6—exclusively homosexual

This scale further complicated the already unreliable demographic guesses concerning the rate of homosexuality. Previously, estimates ranged from 1:1,000 to 5:100 (Ellis, 1961); also, homosexuality was thought to be more prevalent in the female than in the male. Kinsey, however, found that homosexuality occurred more frequently than the quoted figures and was more prevalent in the male. His cumulative, all-embracing index, which even included one single homosexual experience carried to the point of orgasm by the subject up to the age of 45, showed the rate of homosexuality to be 37 percent for all males and 13 percent for all females. When distinct homosexual contacts, as well as those without genital orgasm, were included, the cumulative index rose to 50 percent in the male and 28 percent in the female (Kinsey, 1953). The incidence was higher and rose more steadily with education and was found to be more common in the single and in the urban-dwelling male.

With all due respect to statisticians, who happen to frequently disagree with one another, we can nevertheless conclude from Kinsey's report that homosexuality occurs with considerable regularity. Subsequent statistics, however, as to the actual rise in the incidence of homosexuality in the last thirty years are a matter of debate.

The problem in research is not so much the frequency of homosexuality as the inattention to the relevant subtypes of individuals referred to as homosexuals. The only common denominator in this collective group of people is the single fact that they more or less prefer sexual outlet with members of their own sex. The term *homosexual* says nothing about the route, reason or determinants of how these individuals happen to arrive at a commonly shared sexual behavior. Polarized schools of thought on the psychological and biological causation of homosexuality have been voiced. It appears, however, that, without adequate and scientifically supported subdivision, the issue cannot be validly studied and can be as much an exercise in futility as trying to discern one single cause for an aggregated phenomenon such as headache. Worthy of repeat and emphasis is the fact that behavior of any kind is an interplay between the psychological and biological factors, the two being inseparable in fact. In light of currently available data, it is imperative not only that both factors be considered proportionately but that appropriate subtypes be set up and studied as separate groups.

Earlier descriptions distinguished effeminate and masculine types of male homosexuals as well as masculine and feminine types of lesbians. Social stigmata and popular derogatory names were largely reserved for those homosexuals (and some non-homosexuals because of their appearance) who showed a more or less visible departure from their own respective sexes. Thus, *queen, fairy* and similar unkind terms were used in reference to some effeminate male homosexuals, just as the terms *dyke* and *butch* were reserved for masculine lesbians. Many, but distinctly not all, of these physical features may have been learned or exaggerated. A sharp separation of all homosexuals into these two groups is, of course, unjustified and naive and is widely regarded among homosexuals as a sign of ignorance. How many subtypes and what transitional ranges exist—vital issues from the point of view of research is unkown. The Gay Liberation Movement is of the opinion that homosexuality is a normal variant of sexual behavior, not unlike left handedness. Yet even left handedness derives from three different sources: one that is a normal, harmless variant in the population; another that appears frequently in epileptics and their family members, representing a genetic marker for epilepsy; and finally, the kind that emerges as a result of perinatal minor brain damage.

The study of homosexuals as a solitary group with a single common causation, replicates the problem encountered in schizophrenia research, currently struggling with the same conceptual difficulty. However, the biological reality is under no obligation to follow our simplified and sometimes naive social terminology.

For purposes of the understanding and distinguishing of homosexuals, transsexuals and transvestites, certain characteristic criteria shared by homosexuals must be highlighted.

The homosexual male is attracted more or less exclusively to men and is interested in achieving genital and orgastic satisfaction. He may alternately assume the active or passive roles in the sexual act. Degrees of preference for either of these roles vary individually. Some homosexuals may have an almost exclusive interest in assuming a passive or feminine role, while others place relatively greater importance on providing, rather than receiving, genital satisfaction. Nevertheless, genital orgasm is still important and meaningful and is the reason why sex-change surgery, with the irrevocable loss of the male genitals and physical orgasm, is usually not a tempting proposition.

There is a group of highly effeminate male homosexuals, however, who are interested exclusively in the feminine role and who often have feminine physical features, enhanced feminine mannerisms and a preference for feminine clothing and who may engage in varying degrees of crossdressing. These individuals, set apart from the majority of homosexuals, appear to represent a subvariety with different intensities of fantasies of "being a woman." For a portion of this subgroup, genital pleasure is still an important outlet; others, however, seek transsexual surgery or being to take self-administered or prescribed estrogens. The latter are the individuals who should be most carefully screened before such surgery is recommended. Surgery should always be preceded by one or two years of estrogen administration to produce impotence and feminization—conditions easily reversed by discontinuation of the hormone—and should be accompanied by observation of the individual's response to these events.

Since the advent of the Gay Liberation Movement, homosexuals have experienced more self-confidence in their life-style and their choices, apparently resulting in a reduction of the number of homosexuals wishing to undergo transsexual surgery for less than genuine reasons.

As for the treatment of homosexuality, one should remember that Freud concluded that homosexuality as such is not treatable and that the role of therapy lies in helping the patient to adapt to his sometimes difficult life situation. Most psychiatrists share these views, although a few tend to disagree. Bieber (1962) reported that sexual reorientation could be successfully achieved in one-third of young, masculine-appearing, well-motivated homosexual males with 300 hours of psychoanalysis. Given the many conditions and length of time involved, compared with Kinsey's figures indicating spontaneous reorientation in large numbers of homosexuals (1953), one wonders about the actual magnitude of Bieber's treatment success. What needs emphasis from the point of view of treatment is that homosexuals, like heterosexuals, are subject to all sorts of emotional and mental illnesses and therefore should be dealt with like anyone else. Homosexuality itself may or may not become an issue of the treatment. Psychiatrists should not be crusaders. Sexuality, both heterosexuality or homosexuality, can be practised in either a mature or immature fashion.

Throughout the Western world, homosexuality has always been a shameful secret, evoking the general public's contempt and hatred against male homosexuals in particular, as is evident from the fact that homosexuality used to be a criminal act. Such hostile sentiments were aroused in the heterosexual public partially because homosexuals represented a minority group but mainly because, as psychiatrists maintain, the ubiquitous potential bisexuality of the human was calling for a defense against an indwelling threat. Therefore, the repression, denial and rejection of those who more or less openly practised what was indeed an inner threat present in all can be understood as a defensive maneuver. By rough approximation, the greater the hidden individual threat is in a nonhomosexual male, the proportionately greater is his overt aggression against homosexuals. Frequently, interest and permissive attitudes, even titillation by lesbianism, along with hostility towards the male homosexual, is thought to be a "give-away" sign of latent homosexuality.

Sharing a mutual interest and facing common problems, homosexuals have withdrawn into the isolation of the gay world. Since the beginning of the Gay Liberation Movement, much has changed within and outside homosexual circles. A recent issue of the *New York Times* (1978) published a feature article describing homosexuality on the university campus. The strivings and efforts of the Gay Liberation Movement are public knowledge. Since, however, heterosexuals do not march, wave flags and print slogans, one wonders if the noise made by homosexual organizations will not eventually create an adverse general backlash.

MALE TRANSSEXUALISM

The position of a tiny, distinctly different minority within a larger minority group is always pathetic. Transsexualism, a rare condition, occurs by Wålinder's (1967) estimation in 1:37,000 of the male and 1:103,000 of the female population. Despite the surgical transformation of Christine Jorgensen, reported by Hamburger (1953) and in a brief treatise by Abraham (1931), the condition was fairly unknown except as a rarity until the work of Benjamin (1964, 1966), who has been studying this issue since 1953. The *Index Medicus* did not use a separate listing for this disorder until 1968.

Anatomically a man by currently available biological measurements, but with a distinct core gender identity of a woman, the male transsexual feels, grows up, acts and behaves as closely to the female as he can. Most feminine characteristics come "natural" to him from an amazingly young age. Unlike homosexuality or transvestism, although not invariably, the disorder becomes noticeable in infancy. Clinical reports by Stoller (1966-67), Green and Money (1969) and others describe signs of transsexualism in children as young as two years of age. The infant and early childhood form of male transsexualism is characterized by a natural proclivity in the pursuit of all girlish interests in style of play, playmates, decor and dressing. In spite of their being boys, some transsexuals are reputed to be brought up as girls as the result of a more or less conscious or hidden preference for girls on the part of the mother. Nevertheless, this formulation of the "cause" contains its share of simplification, for many boys exposed to the above mentioned milieu grow up to be heterosexuals, while many transsexuals lacked similar environmental influences in their childhood milieu.

As childhood transsexuals grow, so does their attraction to feminine attire and their compelling desire to "be" a woman. Occasional episodes of crossdressing, in secret with sought-after alibis such as Halloween, parties, school theaters, etc., are easily traceable events in their early history. At puberty, and consistent with their previous development sexual craving for the "same" sex, that is, toward the male will develop. Crossdressing and autoerotic fantasies about males will provide both satisfaction and guilt. Their identity is often described with the by-now platitude, "They are females, locked in a male body." Unlike transvestites, however, they will experience no, or only incidental, sexual arousal by the act of crossdressing. Instead they report a "sense of comfort, relaxation or being natural." Regarding themselves as female emotionally, they recognize that they are not typical homosexuals.

The eventual sexual partner will, of course, be male. Their dreams, hopes and fantasies will be towards a masculine "real" man and not towards a homosexual. Inherent in their situation is the fact that such a "real" heterosexual man will patently reject them. So, by necessity rather than by choice, they will "settle" for a homosexual outlet, but not without frequent bilateral dissatisfaction. Just as the homosexual male does not seek sexual outlet with a surrogate female, neither does the transsexual feel that his emotional needs are satisfied by the homosexual act. The genital, orgastic sexual need of the trans-sexual is typically low. Some, for all practical purposes, are asexual but have a considerable emotional need to assume the "female" sexual role. Their sexual need is to give and to offer sexual pleasure to a male rather than to receive it. Dislike, even hate, of their own male sexual organ is so universal and can reach such proportions that they are driven to self-castration or self-mutilation, an occurrence repeatedly reported in the litera-ture (Pauly, 1968; Stoller, 1973; Glaus, 1952; Lowy, 1971). Transsexuals are beset, if not obsessed, with looking feminine and invent complex practices to learn to hide their sexual organs (Fig. 1-2). The inevitable development of facial or body hair is somewhat of a disaster for them, and they spend hour upon hour plucking or hiding it.

It is common for transsexuals in the early or midteens to secretly wear feminine underwear under their own despised male clothing. They will happily associate with other "normal" girls and engage in "girltalk" and shopping; in fact, so great is their desire to be one of them that they occasionally complain of menstrual cramps. Unlike transvestites, to whom female attire, particularly underwear, has to be exaggeratedly "sexy," if not whorish, and who wear female clothes in order to be sexually aroused, genuine transsexuals prefer actual and con-temporary female fashions, often slacks and attire of the type "other girls wear." They attend male gay bars or homosexual meeting places, but they neither feel nor are made to feel entirely comfortable there. Typically they avoid lesbians.

Other aspects of the personality of transsexuals and homo-sexuals are the same as those found in a cross section of the general population. They may be mature, reserved, "lady-like," seductive, immature, promiscuous, bright or limited, educated or simple, healthy, neurotic or psychotic. Some, in their despera-tion, may attempt suicide; others may find themselves unable

to cope with their complex situation and thus are equally un-
suited to either the heterosexual or homosexual societies. Nevertheless, truly amazing is their determination in facing family
and social complications, which occur more frequently for them
than for an average homosexual, and their endurance in accepting the frustration, pain and costly surgery necessary for the
fulfillment of their ambition.

Transsexualism as previously described is, of course, a
stereotype and occasionally is found in this full-fledged form,
although many variations are possible. For example, crossdressing may not take place until a later age. The entire condition may not manifest itself until middle age. Heterosexual
activity with satisfaction—even marriage, in the past or present—
is not impossible. However, all transsexuals are alike in their
consuming desire and untiring efforts to become surgically
"female" and to be rid of their male sex organ; thus, they differ
from the typical transvestite or homosexual who would abhor
the idea of parting with his pleasure-providing sexual organ.

Rare, scattered and dubious cases of cure by means of various
psychotherapeutic approaches have been reported in the psychiatric literature. However, most authorities agree that the
condition is practically untreatable by any means other than
palliative surgery. Such surgery is performed for four reasons:
the condition is untreatable by other means; surgery can prevent
self-castration; it can prevent suicide; and it enhances emotional
adaptation.

Follow-up studies (Benjamin, 1967; Fisk, 1974; Pauly, 1968;
Randell, 1969; Hoenig, 1971) testify to the fact that a better
emotional adaptation and more normalized life-style result from
surgery. Subsequent to surgery, some transsexuals live a promiscuous life, while others have very limited sexual activity. Some
get married, adopt children and are reportedly good mothers.
Green's (1975) study of children brought up by transsexual and
homosexual couples has, to date, shown no abnormality in their
sexual attitudes. However, continuation of the follow-up study
is necessary before definite conclusions can be made.

BLURRING THE FRONTIERS

With the boundaries between typical transvestism, homosexuality and transsexuality having been so succinctly demar-

cated, the differences hopefully will emerge with clarity. However, once again, a degree of confusion concerning these terms must be introduced by means of the reshaping of these concepts so that they will resemble more closely the actual real-life likeness. Also, at this point the term *spectrum* must be introduced, obfuscating the rigid borders of the definitions and focusing on the overlap existing in some of those individuals who fall into either of the aforementioned categories.

The typical instances of transvestism, homosexuality and transsexuality remain comfortably set apart clinically, permitting an unambiguous diagnosis. Each of the three classes can, nevertheless, present diagnostic problems.

An undefined number of the atypical transvestites eventually may become so obsessed with their own fostered femininity that they are overcome by a desire to be transformed surgically to female. This tormenting obsession is of such magnitude in some that it becomes as consuming as that observed in the true transsexual. Furthermore, sometimes a characteristic fetishist-transvestite case history, upon closer scrutiny, will reveal at least some transsexual developmental features.

It was mentioned that an effeminate, passive homosexual man may sometimes become more preoccupied with his feminine role and appearance, that these ambitions may eventually outweigh orgastic pleasure and that he may be overtaken by a fervent desire for total surgical feminization. Such is the case, in particular, in those homosexuals having both low levels of sexual potency and marked narcissistic self-indulgence.

Some physical sexual practices in all three categories foster and reinforce a psychological feminization. One such indulgence is masturbation to orgasm without an erection.

While the typical fetishist, transvestite and male homosexual will never give up his pleasure-providing sexual organ, the transsexual, the rare atypical transvestite and the effeminate passive homosexual will gladly exchange his usually low sexual potency for the identification pleasure he gains by the complete surgical transformation. Differentiation within that group of people is sometimes a futile academic exercise, which is why the term *gender dysphoria* (Stoller, 1973; Fisk, 1974), an intense displeasure with one's own physical and sexual role, was intro-

Figure 1-1. Advertisement for interested transvestites, including "full theatrical wardrobe, wigs, shoes, boots and makeup lessons."

duced. Patients in this overlapping class of disorder may or may not be suitable candidates for sex-change surgery. Psychotherapeutic efforts are almost always unsuccessful. The surgical solution must be preceded by unhurried and circumspect consideration of a wide variety of conditions other than the rigid implication of diagnostic categories. Such conditions for decision on surgery include the intensity and consistency of the patient's pursuance of the surgical solution after his detailed understanding of its consequences, taking into consideration previous attempts at psychotherapeutic resolution of the problem, physical endowments and suitability for the longed-for gender, personality resources, intelligence and absence of physical and mental illnesses, mental retardation, impulsivity, and psychopathic trends. Social situations, adaptability and future plans in his ("her") new sexual role must also be considered (Koranyi, 1976). Observation of his response to the still reversible estrogen-induced impotence and breast development is usually accompanied by a demand that he live, dress and work as a female for some time before surgery is finally recommended. Absence of sexual relations with a male, in the case of a male candidate for surgery, is an adverse sign, since the psychological adaptation to sexual relations is not dependent on the surgery. The latter point is sometimes rationalized by the patient stating that he will "do so only when he is a complete female." Female impersonators were reported to be poor candidates for sex-change surgery (Roback, 1975).

Much has been written on the issue of what might be "the" cause behind these sexual deviations. Exclusive psychological and genetic-biological etiologies often claim sole validity. But, despite the accumulated knowledge of both the psychological and biological nature of sexuality, a final answer is elusive, despite the accumulated knowledge of both the psychological environmental influences exert a dislocation of the usual sexual development, but only in a biologically vulnerable individual. Some excellent review articles deal with this encompassing issue (Ploeger and Flamm, 1976).

In contrast to transsexuality, the fetishistic-transvestite features may be more decisively influenced by the psychological

Figure 1-2. Technique of hiding the penis used by some transsexuals. Both photographs were taken before surgery. The photograph on the left shows the penis "gaffed." The testicles are pushed up into the inguinal canal, appearing only as a faint shadow under the skin covered by the genital hair. The penis is then bent down and folded over by the empty scrotum. It is held in this position with clear tape. The photograph on the right shows the penis "out."

contributors. The relative degree to which either fetishism-transvestism, homosexuality or transsexuality dominates the life-style of an individual renders the biological research more difficult. Furthermore, each of these conditions represents a common emotional and behavioral endpoint and need not have been brought about by the same cause—a hitherto insufficiently appreciated possibility. Evidently, each case merits a highly individualized approach in the process of evaluation and treatment.

CHAPTER 2

HISTORICAL ASPECTS

Mythology and history are separated by a thin but hazy line of relative credibility. Both reflect enduring human preoccupations and interests and are thus subject to investigation by the behavioral scientist.

Humans, according to Greek mythology, were built from mere clay. They became enviably godlike only when Prometheus breathed Soul into them by means of the flame he had stolen from Olympus, a crime for which he paid dearly. Man, too, had to be punished. The sexist version of the story recounts that Zeus created the first woman, Pandora, who was then endowed with alluring charms by all the gods so that she would destroy man's innocent happiness. But *sex*, from the Latin *secare*, "to cut," has another, more poetic, allusion. The godlike, complete man was cut in two parts—the male and female—by the lightning of Zeus, and a whirlwind ensnared the two in all humankind. Since then, each of these inherently less than sufficient entities has been forever searching for its lost parts; when each finds the other, they embrace for life.

Conceivably, in this "reunion," there are occasional mistakes. The skilled talker and Olympian godly messenger, Hermes, who was also the god of travellers and thieves, together with the delightful, somewhat promiscuous goddess of love, Aphrodite, procreated an illicit son named Hermaphroditos. As related by Ovid, the nymph of the fountain of Salmacis in Helicarnassos had fallen in love with the boy and wished to be forever united with him. The nymph's prayers were answered; when Hermaphroditos quenched his thirst from her fountain, the two of them became one: half man and half woman. Folklore has left for us a few magnificent ancient sculptures: the Herma-

Figure 2-1. The Sitting Hermaphroditus. Antique gem from Sardonyx. Courtesy of the British Museum, London.

phrodite of Polykles, and that of Miracourt, as well as the paintings of Hermaphrodite in Pompeii (Fig. 2-1).

According to Herodotus, Aphrodite apparently had learned a lesson and, in turn, punished the hemp-smoking nomadic Scyths for having plundered her temple in Askalon by inflicting them with frequent impotence, eunochoidism and transvestism. Hippocrates, on the other hand, explains that the Scythian disease was a result of excess horseback riding.

The Old Testament (Deuteronomy 22:5) forbids crossdressing. Surely where there is a law, there is a precedent. The reason for the existence of crossdressing in biblical times is not evident from the Scripture. Besides being engaged in by transvestites, transsexuals and homosexuals, crossdressing might have been done as a means of obtaining an otherwise forbidden, intimate closeness to women, according to certain dimly-lit sources of the Talmud.

All these examples illustrate that sexual ambiguity and sex change did not begin with Christine Jorgensen.

According to Will Durant (1944), the first historically recorded sex-change operation was performed on a man called Sporus, an ex-slave, who subsequently became the wife of Nero, the last Caesar. This strange event took place soon after the tragic death of Nero's beloved, but cunning, wife, Poppaea, in A.D. 65. When the late-stage pregnant Poppaea reproached Nero for having arrived home late from the races, Nero kicked her in the stomach and thus caused her miscarriage and death. The grief-stricken Nero then found Sporus, whose features, to Sporus' misfortune, reminded him of Poppaea. Sporus was castrated and formally married to the by then deranged Caesar. In the absence of a responsible follow-up study on the readaptation of Sporus to his new role, one can only conclude that he did not have time to reach such a state, as Nero died two years later.

Many Roman emperors, including Augustus, Tiberius, Hadrian, Domitian and Trajan, were well-known bisexuals. Julius Caesar was said to be "every woman's man and every man's woman" (Sussman, 1976). Transsexualism, however, was best illustrated in the biography of the Roman emperor Elagabulus (Green, 1969; Benjamin and Masters, 1964). Elagabulus, or Heliogabulus (205-222), whose true name was Varius Avitus and who was thought to be the illegitimate son of Caracalla, dressed and lived as a woman. During his short four-year reign, he kept his body and facial hair depilated and married a male slave. He offered half of his empire to the surgeon who could make him into a woman. He was slain in A.D. 222.

In ancient Greece, and particularly in Rome, female roles in Greek dramas were traditionally played by men dressed in female attire, just as Japan's kabuki dancers were males dressed in women's clothes. This custom, however, was probably not based on transsexuality. Crossdressing presumably occurred in all strata of social classes throughout the ages. Many authors, such as Magnus Hirschfeld and Havelock Ellis, have collected historical accounts of crossdressers. More recent data on the historical aspect of transsexuality was offered by Bullough (1974, 1975).

History often is an elusive love and favorite pastime for some creative minds. Unfortunately, its accurate quotation requires time-consuming references. Green (1969) quotes de Savitsch's (1958) claim that "Pope John VIII who followed Pope Leo IV in 855 A.D. in fact was a woman who died in childbirth." The trouble with de Savitsch's statement is that Pope Leo IV was followed by Benedict III. Pope John VIII, who in fact followed Adrian II in the abovementioned year, appeared to be very much of a man, deeply involved in the complex business of politics and in the threatening Saracen invasion. He was murdered by his conspiring court on December 16, 882.

More accurate is the transsexualism of Abbé de Choisy (1644-1724), who, according to another misled author (Block and Tessler, 1971), was supposed to be the brother of King Henry III of France (1551-1589). Indeed, Green (1969) considers Henry III as having been a potential transsexual. According to de Savitsch (1958), Henry III, the favorite son of Catherine de Medici, made his court address him with the French equivalent of "Her Majesty" and on occasion dressed in female clothes. Although he had indulged in a series of murderous intrigues with his famous mother to whom he was supposed to be extremely close, Henry III exclaimed with joy upon his mother's death, "Now I am a King." Childless when he himself was murdered, the Valois House died with him.

The Abbé de Choisy, who lived approximately 100 years later, was indeed a famous transsexual, although Bullough (1975) does not necessarily classify him as such. De Choisy was brought up as a girl by his mother. His thrill in wearing feminine clothes and in living as a woman is evident from his autobiography as quoted by Gilbert (1926) and Bulliet (1928).

"Éonism," Havelock Ellis' now outdated term for transsexuality and transvestism, derived from the name of the most famous transsexual man of the eighteenth century: Chevalier Éon de Beaumont (1728-1810). He was a secret diplomat and a self-confessed transsexual whose crossdressing became notorious when Louis XV sent him on a diplomatic mission to Russia in 1755, dressed as a woman. Similar missions to London followed. Although a soldier who excelled in fencing, he was so skilled in crossdressing that his true sex was often guessed wrongly and his true male gender was not clearly established until a post-mortem examination. Because of Éon's controversial autobiography three years after the death of Louis XV, he was ordered by Louis XVI to wear female clothes for the rest of his life. Even though Éon no longer lived in France, he apparently enjoyed this agreeable sentence from the French king. Portraits of him in both the male and female roles are featured in the work of Haeberle (1978). Éon's disfavor with Louis XVI was probably based on gossip attributed to Éon that the brother of Louis XV was raised as a girl. Similar rumors had been spread earlier about Prince Phillippe, Duke of Orleans, the brother of Louis XIV.

The Township of Hyde Park, New York, where Franklin Delano Roosevelt was born and buried, got its name from Lord Edward Hyde, Viscount of Cornbury, a governor of New York and New Jersey (1702-1708), who, during his short stay in office, had dressed alternately as a male and as a female. The well-known portrait of him in female attire is on display in the Smithsonian Institution, was featured in the book of Bailyn Davis et al. (1977) and was reproduced in *Time* magazine (April 25, 1977).

More recent was the still questionable gender of the Scottish poet William Sharp (1856-1905), who in 1894, nine years after his marriage to his first cousin, published stories under the pen name of Fiona MacLeod in order to express the feminine side of his feelings.

These historical remarks are intended to demonstrate the existence of a long continuum of male transvestism and transsexualism throughout Western civilization rather than to represent a complete and detailed study of the problem.

CHAPTER 3

SEXUAL DIMORPHISM, NATURAL SEX CHANGE AND ELUSIVENESS OF SEXUAL ROLES IN NATURE

N ATURE'S INHERENT urge to procreate the living could be considered to be the "secret of life" itself, even though its cause remains an unresolved puzzle. Given the appropriate conditions, the chromosomal DNA molecule will multiply. Procreation does not necessarily require union of the two sexes in all species; among plants and other forms of primitive life, the asexual, "unisex" procreation is the rule, with some exceptions. The advantage of asexual procreation for a species is the rapid stencillike reproduction of large numbers of identical daughter cells, well suited to these life forms. Adaptation is a fundamental condition of life. Therefore, a less favorable sequel of asexual development is the lack of exchange of chromosomal material between the cells. This disadvantage, which hinders the mingling of slightly discordant genes, denies, in a relative sense, an opportunity for genetic mutation, and thus patently limits higher ranges of adaptability, which is dependent upon new gene assortment. Separation of a species into two different sexes does, however, occur in many plants. Two-sexed plants were first described in 1694 by the German physician Rudolf Jacob Camerarius. But there is also evidence that Pliny the Elder made mention of them; artificial insemination of male-female palm dates was portrayed in some ancient relics as well.

In contrasting simple asexual multiplication with the higher forms of sexual procreation, it is evident that the latter is better suited for the task of mobility and offers extended adaptational variability. In the evolutionary ascent, some species specialize into male and female forms, the slight overlap between them being referred to as sexual dimorphism. From then on, the maintenance of the male-female sexual division is assured in the species by the transmission of a unique, sex-determining chromosome.

The derivation of the word *sex*, from the Latin *secare*, to cut or divide, reflects the intrinsic incompletion of the single-sexed organisms as far as procreation is concerned. Male and female, proportionate participants in the creation of a new organism through the exchange and sampling of their genetic material, open a wider range of "experimental potential" for nature. Such trial and error, of course, can go either way. More extreme forms in both the favorable and the undesired adaptive directions are created, one thriving, the other doomed.

The evolvement of these viable or deficient extreme variants is continually screened by natural selection throughout the infinite time available to phylogeny. Intermarriage between the carriers of advantageous traits will further strengthen their penetrance and assure their transmission to future generations. Thus, the desirable inherited modalities keep increasing in a species towards a peak—a peak beyond which the benefit of the same heritage may ultimately become a fatal liability leading to the eventual extinction of the species, as was well described by the ethologist Konrad Z. Lorenz (1963).

For at least the duration of the ascent of the species, the demand for procreation is imperatively conveyed to the individual organism by an urging displeasure—the sexual need. The sexual instinct, a quantum of behavioral energy budgeted for that purpose, imposes the necessity for periodic sexual acts. Repeated experiences of satisfaction, bringing sexual "relief," and its anticipation, turn sexual "displeasure" or tension (so called by Freud [1905]) into corresponding and impelling sexual pleasure. The bribe of this satisfaction thus forces the individual to acquiesce with the procreation of the species. The striving to fulfill this latter purpose—one might be tempted to say "design"—for procreation is so important that the natural selection has apparently no interest in extending further protection to members of the species who are beyond the age of reproduction. This is well reflected in the abrupt fall of resistance to certain illnesses, including malignant tumors, once that age has passed.

The evolutionary panorama is all around us. The transitional stages from asexual procreation to sexual dimorphism can be widely observed. Dimorphism, the evolutionary emergence of the sexes whereby a single chromosomal difference determines maleness (XY) and femaleness (XX), begins in such lower species as fish and worms, but at this stage it is still less distinctive and subject to spontaneous reversal.

A few examples will be helpful in highlighting the tenuous nature between male/female sexual differentiation in some species.

In 1876, Hartman observed that the worm *Ophriotrocha puerilis*, when young, is male. Reaching a size of twenty segments, it becomes a female. When two such females are isolated, the one having fewer eggs reverts to being a male and fertilizes the eggs of the other female. In contrast, the Red Sea goldfish is female when young but becomes a male as it grows older (Yamamoto, 1969). The worm *Bonellia viridis* is able to control the sex ratio of its own offspring. It lays some eggs inside and some outside of a small amount of water. When it releases a virilizing hormone into the water, the larvae there become males, whereas those outside the water and thus unexposed to the hormone remain females (Baltzer, 1937).

The marine snail *Aplysia* is hermaphroditic and can serve as either male, female or both when copulating. On such occasions these molluscs often form chains of three to ten animals, in which the first fulfills the exclusive role of female and the last that of male, with those in between complying with both roles simultaneously. Sometimes (Kandel, 1976) they close the chain and form a circle during copulation, which lasts for a considerable period of time.

Fishelson (1970) described an interesting spontaneous sex conversion in the red fish *Anthias squamipinnis*. When exclusively female fish were placed in a tank, one of them became a male. But when the tank was divided by a glass wall into two separate compartments, one containing exclusively female fish and the other containing a single male fish with other females, no such sex conversion to the male sex took place in the females of the first compartment as long as the male fish remained visible to them through the glass.

One may justly ask what humans have in common with fish. In answer, it may be said that we all came from the ocean. We still have remnants of gills, which at times can, in the human, form tumors called branchioma in the branchial arches. Also, despite the chromosomal determination of the human sexual status at conception, our first sexual organ in early fetal development is called the indifferent gonad because of its still inherent potential at that stage to develop into either male or female external genitalia.

Sexual dimorphism is never quite complete in any of the known species (Beach, 1968). Experimental manipulation in animal research and a variety of human pathologies interfering with unambiguous sexual evolvement will be accounted for later. The human male and female, fortunately manifesting remarkably different shapes, nevertheless share considerable overlap.

SEXUAL DEVELOPMENT AND PATHOLOGY OF THE FETUS AND EARLY POSTNATAL PERIOD

The tissues containing the reproductive elements (gametes: the sperm and the ova), the gonads (testis and ovary), as well as the sexual organs reflect a common origin in the human male and female. Not only do the genital organs of both sexes derive from a common, and in the fetus yet undeveloped, genital tissue (the indifferent gonad), but also, in their fully evolved adult forms, they continue to share many corresponding and similar anatomical structures. The loose skin flap, the female labia, bracing the vagina on either side, becomes the male scrotum, fused in the midline by a visible seam, the raphe. The female clitoris, essentially a tiny penis, and the male penis contain erectile tissues supplied by the same pudendal nerve; both end in a tip, the glans, and both are partially encircled by a skin fold, the prepuce. The system of ducts (wolffian and prostate in the male and müllerian in the female) and glands (Cowper's in the male and Bartholin's in the female), as well as the testes and ovaries, are complementary structures. The female urethra, however, is well below the clitoris, while in the male it is located in the glans penis.

The course of fetal evolvement runs along the path of a rigidly maintained timetable. Serial developmental steps must take place at an exact, preset time. The slightest interference with this chemically regulated and extremely delicate process results either in the death of the fetus or in a variety of malformations of the infant. Such malformations include anatomical sexual ambiguity. In the female infant, one of the frequent forms of sexual maldevelopment is the closure of the vaginal opening, labioscrotal fusion. In the male, minor sexual developmental defects include different degrees of malpositioning of the urethra below the usual location, causing hypospadiasis, the severity of which is determined by the extent of the deviance from its expected location. The scrotum, evolving from both sides, may not meet and close in the midline as expected but, as a result of interference with fetal development, may remain partially open, resulting in a urethral slit, a vaginalike opening.

One single chemical interference along the course of fetal unfolding will usually result in a multitude of developmental failures in an infant. These numerous malformations are not necessarily restricted to one particular organ system and are not unlike the case of a bud pierced through with a needle, which shows diverse patterns of widespread damage in the petals of the flower in bloom.

Even more striking is the biochemical relation of the male to the female sexual steroid hormones. These hormones are formed in three different organs: the male testis, the female ovary and the cortical part of the adrenal glands, the latter, of course, being present in both sexes and responsible as well for other more vital functions. All steroids derive from the same master substance, cholesterol, which is formed in the liver from acetate. Under the regulating sequences and rate-limiting control of numerous different enzymes, each altering the cholesterol step by step, a large variety of other substances, including cortisol, aldosterone, and male (androgens) and female (estrogens) sex steroids in various strengths, are produced. The enzymes responsible for the sequential alteration of the original cholesterol are present in the local glandular tissues. The normal presence, abnormal absence or relative insufficiency of such enzymes is determined by genetic inheritance. However, since no enzymes are present for the formation of cortisol or aldosterone in the testis and ovary, these glands will yield sexual steroids exclusively, that is, androgens and estrogens. Androgens, testosterone and other virilizing steroids, as well as many kinds of feminizing estrogens, are created in these three glands.

Both androgens and estrogens are present in each sex, though each has a different predominance. Female orgasm, in fact, is dependent on the production of androgens in the adrenal cortex. Accumulation of undue amounts of virilizing hormones in the woman will result in many changes, including adverse hair growth, menstrual problems, and sometimes altered sexual behavior. An increase of female hormones beyond normal levels in the male will cause reduced potency or impotence, testicular atrophy, female distribution of subcutaneous fatty tissue, loss of body hair and growth of breasts (gynecomastia). Such changes can be the consequence of liver disease, the use of certain drugs or alcoholism (alcoholic feminization syndrome). Androgens are first converted (aromatized) into estrogens in the fatty tissues and hypothalamus and are further broken down in the liver. However, if the liver function is impaired, an aggregation of undue amounts of estrogen may result in consequential feminization of the male. Androgens are the precursors of estrogens; in the female, they are produced in the adrenal gland and in the ovaries.

Peripherally (testis, ovary, adrenal cortex) produced sexual steroid hormones are under the ongoing central control of the pituitary gland, as indeed are most other hormones. In turn, the pituitary gland is subject to the supremacy of certain brain areas. Many different regions of the brain, other than those concerned with accumulated life experiences, memories and learning, are independently and intimately concerned with sexuality. Interconnected and shaping one another's functions, these brain parts contribute decisively to the totality of sexual behavior. The pituitary gland, under complex control, excretes the luteinizing hormone (LH), the follicle-stimulating hormone (FSH) and the prolactin, with the impact on the peripheral sexual glands, sexual functions and secondary sex characteristics.

With respect to hormonal functions, the hypothalamus is a prominently important brain region. Connected upwards with other brain areas and downwards with the pituitary gland, the hypothalamus is as much a brain tissue as it is a glandular organ and thus bridges the brain and the hormonal system. (Fig. 3-1.)

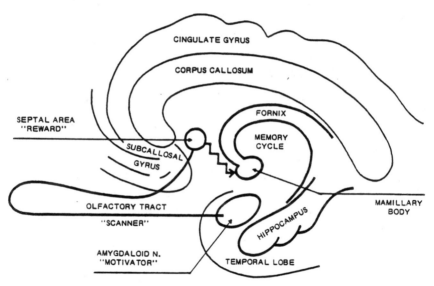

Figure 3-1. Schematic representation of the limbic system.

Urged by still higher-ranking brain centers, the hypothalamus produces minute but measurable amounts of releasing hormones. These releasing hormones are the prerequisites for the activation of other stimulating hormones in the pituitary gland. The peripheral sexual glands (gonads), under the control of the pituitary and the hypothalamus, produce the gonadotropin-releasing hormones (GnRH), which are of particular interest. These hormones are of two kinds and have names representing their functions: the follicle-stimulating-hormone-releasing hormone (FSH-RH) and the luteinizing-hormone-releasing hormone (LH-RH). These substances affect the level of growth, development and maintenance of sexual interest. In one of the many forms of hypogonadism, the lack of or retarded sexual development and reduced sexual interest are related to insufficiencies of these hormones and are reportedly (Reitano, 1975) correctable by replacement therapy.

Distinction has been made between "male" and "female" brains. The differences refer mainly to the hypothalamus and possibly to some other brain areas. The female brain possesses a cyclic quality of function related to the menstrual cycles. Also known is the fact that the hypothalamus is female in fetuses of both sexes until a critical stage. Jost (1959) provided experimental evidence to support the theory that the basic sex is the female one. He castrated male rabbit fetuses intrauterine without interfering with the pregnancy of the mother animal. When this delicate procedure was performed on the nineteenth day of pregnancy, all offspring were born as females. But when the procedure was postponed to the twenty-fourth day, such was not the case and thus was indicative of the occurrence of a critical change during this time span. One of these significant changes is that some of the testosterone-producing Leydig cells in the testis of the fetus convert the fetal hypothalamus from the original female to a male type of tissue due to the high testosterone secretion. The male hypothalamus is acyclic.

A simplified description of the sexually significant hormones and brain functions will be offered here. Subjected to the influence of the hypothalamus and the mentioned releasing hormones, the following pituitary hormones play fundamental roles in physical and behavioral sexuality.

The follicle-stimulating hormone (FSH), present in both sexes and already active in the fetal stage, from the postpubertal period onwards is not as much responsible for the anatomical completion of the genital organ as it is for the exertion of an influence fostering functional maturation and growth of the sexual organs. It maintains the production of sperm. It also brings about the secondary sex characteristics in puberty: deepening of the voice and beard growth in the male, breast development in the female, and growth of pubic hair in both. The isolated absence of FSH in male or female will result in immaturity of the sexual organs, hypogonadism and insufficient development of the secondary sex characteristics. Behavioral sexual immaturity is a frequent concomitant trait. Hypogonadism in the male, if accompanied by a reduced level of FSH and capacity for smell, is called Kallman's syndrome.

The luteinizing hormone (LH) promotes the production of testicular testosterone and ovarian progesterone. In collaboration with the FSH it contributes to the maintenance of secondary sex characteristics. Isolated absence of the LH will result in eunochism similar to that found in the absence of FSH, but fertility may be maintained if no simultaneous impairment of the FSH exists. LH nowadays is used by some as an aphrodisiac.

Likewise, prolactin is present in both sexes, although to date its role in the female has been better recognized. Prolactin in the woman promotes breast development and production of milk. Its excess also reduces sexual urges, enhances motherly behavior in animals (Frantz, 1978) and causes menstrual difficulties. In the male, some forms of impotence are characterized by higher-than-normal levels of prolactin (Horrobin, 1977). Such impotence occurs in prolactin-secreting pituitary tumors and can be helped by surgery or by administration of bromocriptine, which suppresses prolactin levels (Carter et al., 1978).

The primary role of the adrenocorticotropic hormone (ACTH) is the regulation of the rate of conversion of cholesterol to the full range of steroid hormones in the adrenal cortex. Of vital importance is the formation of the carbohydrate metabolism-linked cortisol and the mineral-related aldosterone. ACTH, however, will also stimulate the masculinizing and feminizing types of sex steroids. Sometimes, as a result of a recessively inherited defect, the local enzymes needed for the conversion of cholesterol to cortisol and aldosterone are missing or are available only in a reduced quantity. Depending on the type of the so-affected enzyme, the fetus will either die or be born with a genital defect, an indication of low levels of cortisol. Low levels of cortisol, in turn, will be responsible for high levels of ACTH, an attempt at compensation, but because of insufficient enzymes, ACTH cannot effect cortisol production; instead, the excess ACTH will result in high levels of virilizing sex steroids. The impact on the female fetus will be more severe than the impact on the male. These infant girls will either be born with a visible anatomically malformed genital organ, usually labio-scrotal fusion, or they might be anatomically normal if the condition is less severe. Behaviorally, however, they will show a tomboyish trend and play rough childhood games; in their teens, bisexuality, nymphomania and frequent delinquency will appear. This condition is known as the incomplete form of the adrenogenital syndrome (Simpson, 1976; Grumbach, 1960; Ehrhardt, 1968).

The striking importance of this syndrome is both practical and theoretical. In a practical sense, these young girls will respond well, even behaviorally, to treatment with cortisol (Childs, 1956), which, in turn, will cut down their excess virilizing sex steroids by reducing ACTH levels. It should be reemphasized here that virilizing hormones strongly influence female orgasm. The theoretical importance of this issue is the fact that behaviorally these girls essentially "obey" a biochemical event in their sexual and social relations. This unfortunate condition has been called by some an "experiment by nature."

A still more remarkable observation revolves around a regret-table event preceding the detailed biochemical knowledge of the present time. In the 1940s and 1950s, pregnant mothers, frequently diabetic women, received certain kinds of proges-terone hormones to prevent miscarriage. Some of these proges-terones were found by Bartter (1950) and Wilkins (1958) to have virilizing properties. When these substances were admin-istered before the twelfth week of pregnancy, genital abnormality (labioscrotal fusion) occurred in female offspring. When preg-nant mothers were so treated after the twelfth week of pregnancy, no significant anatomical deviation ensued other than possibly a somewhat larger clitoris. Masculinization of behavior in both the childhood and teenage periods occurred, as did nymphomania, bisexual tendencies and delinquency (Goodman, 1976).

Money and Lewis (1966) studied such girls and described them as intelligent, tomboyish children who rejected dolls, "mothering games" and feminine clothing. Ehrhardt (1968) among others, pointed out that, in their teens, such girls manifest homosexuality in act or fantasy, although few become exclusively lesbian. Some eventually will marry and, with treatment, will be fertile.

Male offspring of pregnant mothers treated with the same progesteronelike substances showed a remarkable several-fold increase of various sexual deviations (Yalom, 1973).

Teratogenic congenital malformations represent a wide variety of abnormalities in the infant that were induced by external means during pregnancy: drugs, chemicals, pollutants, radiation, etc. One such hormone, DES (diethylstilbestrol), not only was used at one time in humans but also is currently being given in large doses to cattle to stimulate higher development and weight gain. Although Canadian law requires that the administration of DES be suspended seven days prior to slaughter, recent evidence indicates that very large doses of such substances are retained in the animal's liver and, if ingested, are transmitted to humans, with unknown consequences to pregnant women. Viral infections may produce the same effect. This vulnerability of the fetus to interferences during pregnancy has been known for some time, especially since the thalidomide tragedy.

The development of the fetus is an extremely sensitive process; its normal course is dependent on the delicate balance and timing of internal biochemical events. All developmental steps must take place within a rigid and narrow timetable. These most sensitive stages can be easily interfered with by innumerable external factors, sometimes with predictable, but often incalculable, consequences. The administration of certain sexual hormones during pregnancy is of the greatest significance to the ultimate sexual evolvement of the offspring. As has been seen, under certain conditions, the effects of such hormones may not only show up as visible anatomical malformations at birth but may also manifest themselves many years later in deranged sexual and social behavior.

Worthy of mention is the fact that a science of "behavioral teratology" does not yet exist. Cases involving the absence of anatomical malformation and the presence of exclusively behavioral abnormality are subject to misinterpretation; a particular sexual behavior may be regarded as the result of early psychosocial influences without consideration of the decisive bio-chemical determinant. What is striking about the incomplete forms and the teratogenic forms of adrenogenital syndrome is the fact that the same pathology existing at a higher level will result in visible anatomical malformation, whereas on a milder level it will produce only behavioral abnormality in one's sexual choices and conduct. Phoenix (1959) proposed that the hormonal constellation in the early stages of fetal development can deter-mine the pattern of a person's eventual sexual behavior in adulthood.

Large amounts of different kinds of sex hormones create diverse sexual maldevelopment, as animal experiments testify. In humans, they need not even be given by a physician but can be produced by tumors in the maternal system. The maternal organism, due to its female hormonal constellation, ceaselessly attempts to feminize the male fetus and is resisted only by his own independent testosterone production (Goy, 1976; Kupper-man, 1967). Yet many nonhormonal agents, such as insecticides and DDT in particular, are capable of reducing testosterone levels (Krause, 1977). Animal research has proven that the mother can be immunized against testosterone. The female off-spring of such mothers were normal despite elevated testosterone levels, but all male offspring were born with sexual malforma-tions (Bidlingmair and Knorr, 1977).

The teratogenic effect of the maternal alcohol intake on human offspring has been studied only recently (Clarren and Smith, 1978) although long suspected. Yet alcohol's effect on the sex hormones (Gordon, 1976) has been well known for some time. Simpson (1976) enumerates nonhormonal agents, including an anticonvulsant, aminogluthatimide, now withdrawn from the market, described by several authors as exerting terato-genic effects resulting in pseudohermaphroditism. He also quotes the work of Wilson and Warkany (1948), who found that low vitamin A levels in the mother resulted in genital abnormality in rats, and that of Selby (1971), who observed that ingestion of wild black cherries caused the same abnormality in pigs.

In light of this knowledge, one justly wonders how many other similar, yet totally unexplored, conditions exist. Who knows how many more hormonal, receptor-linked, enzymatic or genetic abnormalities are still being regarded as sexual "free choices" of the individual based solely on thinking and feeling modalities? How many drugs, food ingredients and pollutants harbor decisive and overriding influences beyond already established biological and psychosocial determinants?

Many other hormones, biochemical agents and neurotransmitters are, of course, involved in the development and maintenance of sexual behavior. Detailed, or even sketchy, descriptions of all of them cannot be provided within the framework of this monograph.

Homosexuality and transsexuality have long been subjects of biochemical and genetic research. Several investigators have explored hormone levels in the homosexual man and woman. This area of research nevertheless is fraught with many difficulties.

The definition of homosexuality is far too ambiguous for the purpose of scientific investigation. Researchers sought to overcome this problem by comparing exclusively homosexual groups of individuals (Kinsey's scale 6) to exclusively heterosexual (Kinsey's scale 0) control groups. The degree to which a particular sexual behavior dominates the lifestyle of an individual is not necessarily the result of biological differences; that is, homosexuals may not constitute a biologically uniform group. Therefore, such comparison may well be similar to that of the proverbial apples and oranges. (Table 3-1.)

Nonetheless, in the last ten years a number of biological studies have been performed, with varying degrees of sophistication and pursuing different research designs and objectives, referable usually to the relative quantity or constellation of sex steroid and pituitary hormone levels in the homosexual male. Some of the more recent studies are summarized in Table 3-I. A similar and more detailed comparison of the literature on this issue was provided by Meyer-Bahlburg (1977).

It is intriguing to note that the majority of these studies, performed in different times and places, did, in fact, reflect some hormonal differences in the exclusively homosexual male groups when compared to heterosexual control groups. These differences were not always concordant, nor were they invariably significant, but the presence of these factors cannot be simply ignored despite the methodological differences, deviance in

TABLE 3-I
SUMMARY OF SOME STUDIES ON SEX HORMONE LEVELS IN THE HOMOSEXUAL MALE

Date	Author*	Nature of Study	Results	Study Samples/Laboratory Technique
1940	Glass, S.J. et al.	Urinary excretion of the ratio androgens:estrogens in homosexual and nonhomosexual males.	Reduced levels of androgens found in the homosexual group.	Form and degree of homosexuality not specified. Available laboratory technique was unreliable at that time.
1970	Loraine, J.A. et al.	Testosterone, epitestosterone and LH levels in homosexuals.	Reduced testosterone and epitestosterone, no change in LH levels.	Small sample size; some not exclusive homosexuals. Laboratory technique criticized (Ryrie, C.G. et al., *Br Med J*, Dec. 12, 1970).
1971	Kolodny, R.C. et al.	Plasma testosterone levels and sperm count in homosexuals.	Significantly reduced testosterone and diminished sperm count in homosexuals.	Reasonable sample size (30 students) stratified as to degree of homosexuality. Sophisticated laboratory technique.
1972	Kolodny, R.C. et al.	Levels of LH, prolactin and FSH.	Elevated LH; no change in prolactin; ambiguous result in FSH levels.	Same group as above.
1973	Margolese, M.S. et al.	Androgen:etiocholanolol ratio.	Reduced in the homosexual.	
1973	Doerr, P. et al.	Plasma estradiol, testosterone, semen.	Some elevation in estradiol; no difference in other parameters.	Mixed group of active and passive homosexuals, from Kinsey 3 to 6 classification.
1973	Birk, L. et al.	Testosterone level changes during psychotherapy of homosexual males.	No correlation found.	Homosexual patients undergoing long-term psychotherapy. Self-selected sample.
1974	Parks, G. et al.	Day-to-day variation of FSH, LH and testosterone levels.	All results within normal.	Small sample size of drug-using juvenile delinquents.
1975	Dörner, G. et al.	Effect of I.V. estrogen on the LH levels in homosexual, bisexual and heterosexual groups.	Reduction of LH levels ("female" brain) in the homosexuals; no change in other groups.	Fair sample size. Sophisticated laboratory technique.
1976	Stahl, F. et al.	Free testosterone levels vs. total testosterone levels in homosexuals.	Significant reduction of free testosterone; no change in total testosterone.	Good sample size. Sophisticated laboratory technique.

* Full citations for all publications given in the Bibliography.

research design and small sample size. A well-controlled investigation with a significantly large number of homosexual individuals has not been performed to date.

Strikingly, more definitive hormonal and behavioral studies of animal homosexuality are available. Induction of homosexual behavior in various species of male and female animals is reliably documented. Even more extraordinary is the finding that the species-specific rate of homosexuality can be freely influenced by hormones (Dörner, 1975, 1976), chemicals such as p-chlorphenylalanine (Gawienowski, 1971), diet such as low tryptophan (Fratta, 1977) and even by the quality of light (Sharma, 1977).

Extensive bisexual behavior of rodents throughout their lives, peaking in their youth, had already been reported (Beach, 1942). Similar observations on hamsters were made by Goy (1968) and on rhesus monkeys by Goy and Phoenix (1971). Goy (1976) concluded an inverse relationship concerning the frequency of male and female bisexuality and stated that the more pronounced homosexual activity is among males in a primate group, the less pronounced it is in the females. He presumed that this phenomenon hinges upon prenatal hormonal conditions.

Abundant animal experiments prove the fact that adult sexual behavior can be easily manipulated by various hormone administrations, either during pregnancy or shortly after birth to the neonate. Prompted by the recent reemergence of research on hormones and behavior (Sachar, 1976; Sandler and Gessa, 1975; Itil, 1976; Goy and Goldfoot, 1975), further reviews of this question were recently provided by Reinish (1976) and Meyer-Bahlburg (1977). For instance, female rats treated postnatally with testosterone for a short period of time will assume a quasi-male type of copulatory pattern (Sachs et al., 1973); with continued treatment, an indistinguishable male pattern of sexual behavior can be permanently established in these female rodents (Meyerson et al., 1973). Male animals treated with testosterone for a short time during the mentioned period will display enhanced aggression for life.

The natural degree of masculinity among apes, paralleling their leadership hierarchy, is remarkably concordant. Less masculine male specimens will be accepted only marginally in the midst of the female group; they will be "peripheralized" and will show an observably higher rate of homosexuality among themselves (Goy and Goldfoot, 1976). Progesterone administration will reduce the sexual drive in female rhesus monkeys (Baum, 1977) and in rodents (Morin, 1977). Late-pregnancy rats exposed simply to ongoing environmental stress gave birth to somewhat feminized male offspring (Dahlöf et al., 1977).

Well recognized is the fact that animal research and behavior cannot be easily translated to, or equated with, human behavior. For this reason alone, all the quoted experimentations would be much less meaningful were it not for the fact that similar "experiments by nature" or the unfortunate results of hormonal treatments to pregnant humans have resulted in outcomes comparable to those observed in animal research.

Further complicating biological explorations of sexual disorders is the fact that even a short duration of hormonal exposure during the fetal or early postnatal period may have far-reaching consequences much later in the life of the offspring. Such hormone exposure may be direct, the result of purposely provided hormone treatment, or indirect, the result of inadvertent exposure to chemical agents, pollutants, or nonhormonal medications that unintentionally alter the hormonal balance during critical developmental stages. When such hormonal imbalance occurs at an already advanced stage of pregnancy or on less than a full-scale measure, observable anatomical malformations are not the result. Instead, the outcome is the eventual emergence of an unconventional sexual modality that is only imposed on the offspring many years later. In the absence of gross pathology, such sexual behavior might be hastily and superficially concluded to be merely a personal "choice" related solely to the psychosocial milieu. The consequences of weak hormonal exposure during the fetal stages of development were demonstrated by Soulairac (1978) when he briefly exposed neonate male rat pups to estrogenic hormones and thus produced impotence in 50 percent of the so-treated animals.

It is easy to get lost in the vast clinical and research material of this question in spite of the full knowledge that the final answers are yet to come.

PSYCHOBIOLOGY OF THE PROCESS OF
MOTHERING—HUMAN AND ANIMAL

Commonly held is the misconception that once the umbilical cord has been severed after birth, the biological link between mother and offspring has been terminated, and that therefore all subsequent events must be exclusively psychological and social in nature. Nothing is more remote from the truth. Mother and offspring, although no longer physically connected units, continue to influence one another both biologically and behaviorally. Mothering, therefore, represents not only a psychosocial but also a biochemical experience, which results not only in the gradual acquisition of emotive-adaptive behavior patterns but also in permanent morphological changes in the offspring. Furthermore, the biochemical influence affects not only the infant but, in fact, both the offspring and the mother who have a multicyclic biological relationship. Too little consideration has been given to date to the ways in which the infant, through active behavior, brings about hormonal, and thus behavioral, changes in the mother.

High maternal pituitary prolactin levels subsequent to birth will induce excretion of milk. Gentle stimulation of the nipples (Kolodny, 1972) by sucking will maintain high levels of maternal prolactin and thus milk production. Prolactin, however, exerts other vital influences on the mother that are beneficial to the infant: it will suppress maternal sexuality and enhance "motherliness" (Frantz, 1978; Kupperman, 1966-67). Thus, the active sucking style of the offspring will bring about hormonal and behavioral changes in the mother suitable to the offspring's needs (Koranyi, 1976). Additionally, high levels of maternal prolactin are caused by the elevation of the pituitary gonadotropin-releasing hormones (GnRH), which, excreted in the milk ("milk GnRH"), in turn influence the induction of LH and FSH levels in the offspring and thus enhance his/her own sexual development, a discovery made by Tallie Baram and co-workers in the Weitzman Institute (1977). Thus, sufficient postnatal masculinization and feminization of the offspring's hypothalamus depend upon the ultimate sucking style of the offspring. Overly vigorous and painful sucking will result in maternal rejection, adverse hormonal and behavioral changes in the mother animal and the denial of all these important advantages to the infant. Such natural rejection on the part of the mother animal takes place just around the time the offspring's teeth begin to break through; attempts to suckle will earn increasingly more kicks than milk, forcing the offspring into the next stage of development and into eventual independence. Concordant hormonal, if not necessarily behavioral, alterations were found in humans (Barchas et al., 1978).

Separation of the young from the mother at a sensitive age results in severe consequences in both humans and animals. As little as a two-hour separation of the rat pup from the mother results in a 50 percent reduction of the enzyme ornithin-decarboxylase, a rate-limiting substance involved in the formation of the RNA and brain proteins (Butler, 1978). Butler has demonstrated that the maintenance of a high level of this vital enzyme in the rat pup's heart and brain is dependent upon the active maternal behavior, that is, her licking and handling of the pup. A three-hour separation will result in a significant decline of the LH level, this substance being responsible for the pup's sexual-hormonal awakening and development (Baram, 1977).

During the immediate postpartum period many nutrition-linked factors will influence the offspring. It is not a coincidence that breast-fed human infants are less likely to suffer infectious diseases (Mata et al., 1971). Remarkably, one might also say, in concordance with nature's effort to protect the offspring, the milk composition does not change significantly with the deprived economic and nutritional status of the mother. However, ethnic variations in the composition of human milk (Lönnerdal, 1976) do occur. Furthermore, at least in the cow, maternal stress, noise levels, and air pollution bring about the widest variety of hormonal fluctuations; the levels of prolactin, growth hormone and cortisol are affected (Johnson et al., 1976), altering the composition of the milk and presumedly influencing the offspring (Dahlöf et al., 1977). Human infants of diabetic mothers often develop hypoglycemia soon after birth (Kalhan, 1977; Haworth, 1976; Gabbe, 1977). Since maternal glucose represents the prime source of nourishment for the infant, such early hypoglycemias are of some consequence.

The effect of the environment in which the infant lives his/ her early life can also exert lasting biochemical and structural changes. Bennett, Diamond, Krech and Rosenzweig (1964) were the first to demonstrate in a series of studies that infant rats developed and matured differently in different milieu. Rat pups raised in a challenging, colorful and stimulating milieu, when compared to those brought up in a drab, restricted environment, showed, weeks after their birth, a 30 percent greater brain weight, higher sexual maturity and higher levels of brain bound enzymes and chemicals (acetylcholine, acetylcholine-esterase, hexokinase and protein) (Bennett, 1973). They also showed larger amounts of cortical and subcortical gray matter. When such "superior" animals were interbred, it was found that they transmitted these higher developmental achievements to their offspring. Greenough et al. (1973) confirmed these findings and also found enhanced complexity of certain brain cells (dendritic changes) in various parts of the cortex, a finding previously described by Schapiro (1970). Even a brief exposure to a challenging "enriched" milieu (Henderson, 1975) was sufficient to promote some of these changes, to a degree. Certain depressant drugs, on the other hand, were found to adversely affect brain development (Bennett et al., 1973).

In contrast, visual deprivation (Hubel and Wiesel, 1959, 1970) or manipulation of the visual field (Pettigrew, 1972; Lund, 1972; Hirsch, 1970; Nelson, 1975) resulted in permanent underdevelopment of certain brain areas (Glass, 1973; Kolata, 1975).

This selected sample of information is intended to convey to the reader the infinite complexity and the potential biological vulnerability of sexual development.

Still other observations reveal the vital importance of the mother's presence in early human infancy. Because of the work of Spitz (1951), a devastating depression, capable of occurring in the human infant, is now a well-known form of pathology. Such anaclitic depression, ensuing in a six- to eighteen-month-old human infant upon separation from its mother, can be life threatening and the cause of severe and permanent damage. Subsequently, evidence from Harlow's experiments (McKinney,

1975) further demonstrated a similar point. Monkeys brought up by inanimate mother surrogates, after having been separated from their natural mothers at birth, developed severely mal-formed behavior patterns with a striking absence of social and sexual maturation. Although the extensive data produced by Harlow cannot be presented here, the simultaneous retardation in the biological and psychosocial modalities of these apes must be highlighted.

PSYCHOSOCIAL MODIFICATION OF SEXUALITY

Biology and psychology being inseparable, it is not surprising that this discussion should lead to the psychological aspects of development. The flow of subtle and two-way messages between infant and mother represents the earliest input to the eventual feeling and thinking modalities of the offspring. The mother, a fully grown product of her society, culture and subculture, willingly or unintentionally transmits to the infant conscious or hidden formative hints of all sorts. These messages reach and teach the infant at a time when his/her sole concern is the comfort that can only be provided by the mother and by mothering. Not unlike a flower turning its face to the life-giving sunshine, the infant opens his/her total receptiveness towards the positive and negative expressions of the mother. The assem-bly of these communication fragments will meet and mingle with his/her biological resources, and the unique alloy of the two determines the course of a long road, the direction in which it leads becoming evident only much later.

Once the infant gathers a sufficient quantum of perceptions and attains stages of biological maturation, ostensibly the psychosocial factors and gradually learned behavior gain a relatively higher degree of importance.

Many psychological systems have evolved, each intended to provide a comprehensive grasp of the development of the mind, personality and sexuality. However, most of these psychological theories emerged historically, before the current development of modern neurosciences and biological discoveries. Many of these discoveries have been only partially or insufficiently assimi-lated by these psychological schools. The basic tenets of these

theories having preceded the recent scientific results, these
theories understandably contain a proportionate share of unsup-
ported, and sometimes contradictory, speculations. Devout
followers of such psychological systems often display an enduring
loyalty to earlier great thinkers, whom they revere as founders
of their respective schools, forgetting that in science, loyalty
and adherence are not virtues but sins. Life is more complex
than simplified cause-and-effect models. Appropriate, therefore,
is Abraham Maslow's (1966) observation: "When the only tool
you have is a hammer, it is tempting to treat everything as if
it were a nail." Each of these schools attempts to explain human
behavior exclusively in accordance with their own models.

It was said that "cause is not a chain, but a net" (Browne,
1951). Many of these psychological systems offer valuable and
relevant contributions to our knowledge of human behavior.
The modern understanding of behavior is at its best when it
freely samples the products of all theories and retains a high
degree of conceptual mobility.

Currently dominant major psychological systems are the
psychoanalytic, psychodynamic or "instinct" theories of Sigmund
Freud and the learning theories of Pavlov and his followers.
The original founders of these theories, who are often set into
opposition with one another, have more or less freely admitted
that in the absence of sufficient neurophysiological and hormonal
"details," it was the "entity" of the behavior that formed the
subject of their studies. Both schools, nevertheless, proclaim a
biological foundation.

The biological root of the psychoanalytic school is based
on the assumption that there are two kinds of psychic energies—
sexual instincts and aggressive instincts—and that all human
behavior is motivated by one or the other instinct. These
instincts are operant from birth onwards, and through stages
of development and modification in the attainment of pleasure,
the individual matures emotionally, sexually and culturally.
Despite the fact that Freud repeatedly wrote of the significance
of the then little-known factor of "constitution" (which in
modern terms could be equated with developmental genetics),
his followers placed lesser importance on it and thus forced a
wedge between the psychological and the biological aspects of

human behavior. However, introduction of the concepts of psychosomatics in the 1940s established a narrow bridge between the two orientations.

The behaviorism of J. B. Watson was a forerunner of learning theories, which were based on Pavlov's research on conditioned reflexes. Because of the refinements of Skinner, Miller and many others, later learning theories have had a distinct and deeper biological orientation. Acquired behavior patterns, thought to be reinforced by reward and deterred by punishment, were the base concepts upon which these theories have been built.

The simplest definition of the two systems is that of the prominent neuroscientist Arnold Mandel (1976), who stated that "psychiatric philosophers fall into two camps: those who feel that the music of life comes before the words, and those who feel that the words precede the music."

Psychoanalytic theories propose the existence of a psycho-sexual line of development taking place from early childhood onwards, whereby growth occurs in a preset sequence of oral (from birth to approximately 2 years), anal (2 to 4 years) and oedipal or phallic (4 to 7 years) stages, followed by a latency period (8 to 12 years) and finally a mature genital stage. The acquisition of typical personality traits is supposed to be dependent upon the successful resolution of each of these stages and on the identification processes with the parents. A "fixation," or breakdown of the psychosexual development, is a possible event at any of these stages due to binding conflicts, with a resultant impairment of the personality structure. In the case of homosexuality, such a presumed fixation was thought to be particularly significant from the anal stage to the latency period (Fenichel, 1945). Some psychoanalysts, particularly Socarides (1970), equated transsexuality with homosexuality.

Learning theories are more symptom oriented than psycho-analytic theories. Behavior or symptom is thought of as an individual admixture of adaptive and maladaptive learning, conditioning and reinforcement. The accumulated mass of parental, social and peer expectations, encouragement, rejection and patterns of approval-disapproval (essentially varied degrees of reward and punishment) is considered to be the formative and learned influences that map out the course of general development. These guideposts of growth need not be overt and out-spoken messages but can consist of a series of subtle or refined hints. Just as instincts represent the basic tenet of psycho-analytic theories, so are learning theories based upon memory and association processes. Psychoanalytic and learning theories, long considered to be of opposing camps, have fortunately begun to intermingle to bring about an ultimate better understanding of human behavior.

However, neither psychoanalytic nor learning theories, even when combined, provide entirely satisfactory explanations of transsexualism or homosexuality. Transsexualism can occur at a very early age, the first signs of it having been observed in a one-year-old, with quite frequent presentation in two-year-old infants, as reported by Stoller (1968) and Lebovitz (1972). This young age clearly precedes the proposed period of identifi-cation presumed by psychoanalysts. At that early age, the male child in particular is still thought to be part of a mother-infant bond, with a relative emotional distance even to the father or to other identifiable male objects. Furthermore, neither theory can easily be reconciled with the recent observations of Richard Green (1978), who studied the sexual development of thirty-seven children between the ages of three to twenty who were brought up by transsexual and homosexual (both sexes) parents. In thirty-six of these children, their development has entirely matched their actual sex; the thirteen oldest have already had erotic fantasies or overt sexual behavior of a heterosexual orienta-tion. Only one child, a three-year-old boy, has expressed that "he wishes to be a mommy when he grows up." Obviously neither identification nor learned subliminal signals were of significance in these cases, since these children did not acquire the sexual confusion or ambiguity of their parents.

Lacking satisfactory psychosocial models, those dealing with transsexualism have had to rely on the findings of researchers and clinicians who have studied the psychological development of children suffering from genital malformations or from herm-aphroditism. Money and his co-workers have pioneered in this field since the mid-1950s (Money, 1955; Hampson, 1955; Money et al., 1955). They promoted the concept of gender identity, a model that presumed the early imprinting and the firm establishment of a sense of belonging to either the male or female sex (Money et al., 1957). Robert Stoller (1964, 1968) transposed onto Money's transsexuals findings on hermaphrodites and genitally malformed children and proposed the existence of a core gender identity—the inner recognition of sexual belonging. The anatomical sex and core gender identity are not necessarily discordant in the homosexual male but are definitely so in the transsexual male. Consequently, the transsexual feels that he is a "female locked in a male body." In Stoller's termiology, core gender identity should be separated from the concept of sexual role, the latter being an age-appropriate manifestation of sexual behavior. Stoller views transsexualism as being subject to parental influences. Of these influences, he separates four factors as bearing major etiological importance: (1) mother's belief that the child is "beautiful"; (2) extreme and prolonged physical closeness—touching, hugging and cuddling; (3) latent bisexuality of the mother, who had a history of tomboyishness but also a "clear streak of femininity"; and (4) a physically absent or psychologically distant father.

To what degree these psychological factors are present among transsexuals is not easily answered. Certainly, many transsexuals had early childhood histories that precluded the existence of these factors. For others, these factors were prevalent. Even more questionable is the degree to which Stoller's four factors concerning the psychosocial milieu of the infant can be regarded as etiologically decisive, or even universally significant, in transsexualism. Bieber (1977) disagrees with Stoller's "symbiotic" theory. Nonetheless, Stoller's warning that femininity in boys should not be dismissed as a "passing phase" is to be taken seriously. Similar unfavorable prognostications were voiced by Lebovitz (1972) concerning young people with gender identity problems.

NEUROPHYSIOLOGY OF SEXUALITY

No review of sexuality would be complete without a discussion of some aspects of brain function in relation to sexuality. Evidently, such a discussion can be presented only with much simplification and many generalizations. Earlier in this chapter, the vital importance of adaptation in the maintenance of life was stressed. Such adaptation must take place continually and in two directions: inwardly, towards our own bodies, and outwardly, towards the world around us. In both dimensions of adaptation the brain maintains an ultimate supremacy.

Inwardly, the forever changing metabolic, glandular, vascular and tissue needs of the body are met through the autonomic nervous system, the highest centers of which are located chiefly in the hypothalamus. Not only are ongoing domestic body regulations being adjusted at this primitive level of neuronal organization, but also a suitable, task-oriented internal biological state is being created. Thus, the hypothalamus acts as a sort of "channel selector" and attunes the humoral and nervous system so that it can provide the optimal internal state for carrying out the enterprise ahead: sexual activity, food acquisition and intake, physical or mental exertion, relaxation, sleep, etc. Nevertheless, the hypothalamus is essentially inwardly oriented and primarily concerned with the inward adaptation. The different tasks, each demanding a very different constellation of chemical and neurological balances, represent the main function of this brain part, which is well suited to its role, since it is both brain and glandular tissue. This chemical-neurological attunement of the hypothalamus is somewhat mechanical and does not carry the integrated emotional component befitting the task ahead. Such was well demonstrated by old and new explorations (Bard, 1928; Hess et al., 1943; Kaada, 1972) concerning "sham rage." After surgical separation from higher brain areas, the hypothalamus (stimulation of the dorsomedial nucleus, or else destruction of the ventromedial nucleus) produced a somatic readiness in the cat to fight (expressed by hissing, curving of spine, dilation of pupils, rise in blood pressure, piloerection, protrusion of claws) without, however, the appropriate accompanying emotion of anger.

Basic crude emotion, which one might call the animal part of the human (or the Freudian Id), is largely linked with a brain area, the limbic system, which supercedes the hypothalamus, its mechanical autonomic hormonal and regulatory centers. The limbic system, first described as being pertinent to the basic emotions by Papez (1937) and MacLean (1955,

1970), can be viewed as a more outward-oriented organ. Whereas the hypothalamus is concerned with the inward-directed somatic mechanisms of feeding-digesting, bodily sexual functions and neurochemical readiness to fight, the limbic system is geared more for acquiring food, finding sexual partners and tracing enemies in the milieu, while retaining a dominance over the hypothalamic functions. Since the human animal is a sniffing, scanning predator at the limbic levels, it is not surprising that these limbic structures bear a close relationship to the nerve of smell, the olfactory tract, and connected brain areas (rhinencephalon). The smell of food, sex and the enemy represent a predator's chief stimulation. The limbic system is immensely complex and, by necessity, can be described only superficially, by means of simplified terminology of the author's choice (Fig. 3-1).

The limbic system can, for functional purposes, be divided into four parts: (1) the "motivator," (2) the "scanner," (3) the "reward center," and (4) the memory cycle. Of these, only the first demands further elaboration.

The "motivator" (amygdala, an almond-shaped structure in the tip of the temporal lobe) provides the bulk of motivation, that is, the instinct for three kinds of behavior: the aggressive drive, the sexual urge and feeding behavior. Long before the neurophysiology of this structure was described in detail, Freud correctly assumed the existence of two of the three basic instincts. The kind of aggression bound to the amygdala would, in predator terms, represent fight, flight and fright responses (basolateral part). Interestingly, this part of the amygdala, which is pertinent to aggression, is in an antagonistic relationship with that portion of the structure (corticomedial) which relates to sex. This antagonism is of great clinical importance. If the portion relating to aggression is surgically removed (Klüver-Bucy operation), a state of reduced aggression, lack of fear, hypersexuality, abnormal forms of sexuality and enhanced feeding urges will ensue. The animal's leadership qualities and territorial imperatives will be sacrificed as well. In contrast, in cases of temporal lobe epilepsy (abnormal electrical discharges), enhanced and unmotivated aggression and violent behavior will often be associated with hyposexuality or abnormal sexuality

(Blumer and Walker, 1975). Still other areas in the amygdala relate to normal and abnormal food intake. Thus, the functions of the amygdala revolve around the normal and abnormal behavioral modalities of fight, flight, fright, food and sex. The amygdala was referred to as a "motivator" since the aforementioned behavioral qualities at that level are not merely mechanical, as they are in the hypothalamus, but are accompanied by emotions and many rudimentary social elements, well described by ethologists such as Konrad Lorenz. These social elements include territoriality and ritualized fights in relation to aggression, grooming behavior associated with sexual activity, and pecking order in relation to feeding behavior.

Tissue pathologies of the human amygdala result in a variety of behavioral alterations, including transvestism (Hunter et al., 1963; Hooshmand et al., 1969; Davies, 1960), fetishism (Mitchell et al., 1954), aggression (Blumer, 1975; Goldstein, 1974), hyposexuality (Blumer and Walker, 1975) and other abnormal behavior (Hoenig et al., 1960; Hierons, 1966). Therefore, temporal lobe and amygdaloid disorders are of great interest to psychiatrists, neurologists and members of the legal profession.

Another structure in the limbic system is the "scanner," which, of course, is the smelling apparatus, consisting of the olfactory tract and connected brain areas. Although the ability to smell is actually underdeveloped in the human, behavioral and emotional connotations of the smelling apparatus remain of considerable importance. The olfactory tract, is connected to two areas of our present concern: the already mentioned "motivator" (amygdala), via the lateral olfactory stria, and the "reward area" (septal nuclei), via the medial olfactory stria. The "scanner" is the structure that picks up the scent of sex, food and the enemy from the milieu, triple concerns of the predator.

The "reward center," described by Olds and Milner at McGill University (1954), is located in the midportion of the brain, the septal area, which, if stimulated, provides a substantial sensation of pleasure. In animal research, when a tiny implanted electrode stimulates this part of the brain by means of a connected lever that closes the electrical circuit, the animal will literally become addicted to this self-stimulation and will pull the lever up to

5,000 times a day. Under normal conditions, satisfaction of the basic needs will produce electrical discharges in the septal nuclei, although such discharges are not as strong as those produced under research conditions.

In this schema, the last essential part of the limbic system is the memory cycle (the mamillary body and the hippocampus), connected by the fornix on both sides, where learned memories are stored.

How then does adaptive behavior take place, and what is its outcome in the limbic system? The forever urging "motivator" keeps the essential striving for food and sex and the ability to cope with enemies very keenly alive. The "scanner" picks up the environmental, usually olfactory, clues (pheromones) pertinent to these modalities. Whenever the need in question has found satisfaction by trial and error, the reward center fires and pleasure is experienced. The circumstances under which such pleasure has occurred are then stored in the memory Repeated satisfaction of the same kind of reinforcement of the original experience leads to the formation of conditioned reflexes. The route of maladaptive behavior is essentially the same, except for animals in nature, the consequences of such behavior being different than in our permissive society. In nature, survival is reserved for the fittest.

The limbic system and the crude emotions it produces in turn are under the hierarchical dominance of a still higher brain area, the neocortex, which screens, modifies and alters behavior even further by means of specialized cortical areas working in synchrony with modalities of refined judgment and acquired culture of different kinds.

Sexual pathologies may thus ensue from disturbances at all levels of brain organization. At the highest level of the neocortical hierarchy, excess cultural inhibitions resulting from environmental influences may obliterate even socially accepted forms of sexual release, which nevertheless, sooner or later, will invoke a habituation at the lower limbic levels. Another disturbance at the highest neocortical level, consisting of tissue destruction, results in the appearance of unscreened primitive behavior with judgmental impairment. At the limbic system level, aggression or sexual urges may be created by drugs or tissue pathology to a degree too powerful to be screened out by the neocortex. Disbalanced motivational pressure by abnormal electrical discharges, such as in the case of temporal lobe epilepsy, may lead to uncontrollable aggressive or sexual behavior. Hypothalamic impairment may interfere with the essential metabolic, hormonal or autonomic mechanisms relating to normal sexual functioning.

REGRESSIVE SEXUALITY

This discussion has centered on the potential biological frailties and possible psychological infirmities that may occur along the progression of sexual development. Normal sexuality, however, does not necessarily carry a lifelong guarantee; it can be a perishable commodity. Distressed by innumerable physical, toxic or psychological stressors, for practically any age group, customary and conventional sexual behavior may change and manifest itself in an unexpected or dislocated fashion for reasons other than purely free choice. Such a regression may be a transient or permanent event in a person's life. Two categories of such changes should be distinguished.

In certain instances, sexual impairment or altered sexual behavior may represent a nonspecific response to physical or psychological stress. Such regressed, disorganized or otherwise unusual behavior, often in sharp contrast with the person's customary sexual conduct, may be a time-limited single event, a temporary, sporadic or permanent manifestation. Single or sporadic homosexual outlets, for instance, are not unusual incidences in the adolescent; they may also occur under the influence of alcohol, during drug indulgence or as a result of group encouragement, seduction or experimentation. Homosexuality frequently appears temporarily in jails where no sexual partner of the opposite sex is available. Such prison homosexuality may be a transient episode or may become a permanent pattern, depending on the age of the individual, the underlying sexual orientation, and the duration of exposure to this milieu. Transsexuality, however, is not manifested under such conditions. States of depression, a variety of physical illnesses and some medicinal drugs may cause a simple, usually fleeting, decline of sexual needs without any sexually compensatory urges. However, during prolonged states of stress accompanied by degrees of disorganization abnormal sexual urges may be manifest temporarily. In prepsychotic or psychotic disintegration, sexual aberrations, usually of a transient nature or single, often bizarre, events may represent a nonspecific symptom. Thus, indiscriminate sexual behavior in mania, in generalized organic brain damage or in toxic conditions can often be regarded as the nonspecific product of the illness.

The determining of sexual behavior involves a triangular relationship between the modalities of (1) judgment and social skills, (2) sexual urge (libido) and (3) sexual potency. Disharmony between these factors often leads to disturbed sexuality.

With sexual urge and potency unimpaired but judgmental and social skills insufficiently developed (which is the case with young mentally retarded males), a range of aberrant sexual behavior is possible. This may sometimes result in rape, but it more often is manifest in exhibitionism, pedophilia and homosexuality. Crossdressing, however, is a rare occurrence under these conditions. Similarly, in cases of organic impairment of the brain function with reduction of the judgmental capacity, indiscriminate sexual acting out can occur, frequently in the form of heterosexual or homosexual incest. Alcoholic or toxic organic brain impairment, as well as presenile or senile dementias, can also result in such behavior.

Reduced potency or impotence with the sexual urge remaining at a high level might result in a wide variety of sexual and behavioral problems. This is the case with diabetic sexual impairment (Koranyi, 1979). A sizeable portion of the population suffering from known or undiscovered diabetes mellitus will also suffer from impotency, which may be the first symptom of the illness during its gradual development over a period of years. However, despite declining potency, the sexual urge remains high and requires some kind of compensatory behavior. A person under such conditions may, in a marital situation (Koranyi, 1978), display alibi-seeking or blaming behavior and will sometimes reach out for sexual stimuli that, due to their novelty or bizarre quality, can still provide sexual excitation. Regressive sexuality, exhibitionism, homosexuality and transvestism often represent such compensatory efforts. Similar behavior may ensue in cases of temporal lobe epilepsies or in certain specific organic brain syndromes.

CHAPTER 4

GENETICS AND SEXUALITY

A FEW YEARS ago, it would have been a much simpler, but far less exciting, proposition to write a brief chapter on the topic of genetics and sexuality. Today, with final answers still remote, the task has grown into a major challenge. By the time this monograph is printed, its information may well be outdated, since knowledge of medical and behavioral genetics is increasing at a phenomenally accelerated rate.

Heredity and transmission of physical and behavioral proclivities in animals and humans have been known, or at least suspected, since prehistoric times. The Old Testament displays liberal hints concerning this ancient preoccupation. The immortality of the flesh, inoculated from one generation to the other, representing a kind of survival, is probably behind the tenacity with which mankind pursued this interest. Paralleling age-old wisdoms notwithstanding, much naivety and many superstitions prevailed as well concerning the mystery of the way in which the sex of an offspring is determined. Probably Alkmaion, in the sixth century B.C., was the first—if there was a first—to propose that the "larger amount of material" provided by one of the parents decides the sex of an offspring. Thinkers of ancient times—Democritus, Empedocles, Aristotle, to mention an arbitrary few—had a variety of theories on the conditions responsible for the ultimate sex of the infant. The "temperature of the womb," the "quality of the blood" and the "strength and concentration of the semen" were alternate hypotheses at different times. Democritus (460 B.C.) stated that the eventual human being "in a miniature form is represented in the semen." Becker's sexual adviser (Becker, 1807) suggested that the aiming of the stream of semen at the left ovary during intercourse would result in female offspring, and semen aimed to the right would create the male. Maupertuis, the French mathematician (who died some fifty years before that date in the same city where Becker's work was printed), had already talked about "hereditary particles." Similarly, spermatozoa and ova had been described in 1677 by Anton van Leeuwenhoek, a Dutchman, who also discovered the microscope. The latter's contemporary and compatriot Regnier de Graaf gave an account of the ovarian follicles (Graafian follicles) as well as the fact that conception consists of the union of the sperm with the egg.

The turn of the nineteenth century was an excited time in the scientific world. Jean Baptiste Lamarck (1801) proposed his theories of the evolution of the species and forwarded the idea of the inheritance of acquired characteristics. Though he died blind and in great poverty, he created havoc on the scientific and political scenes. Marx and Engels were confirmed Lamarckians; his theories still occupy a prominent place in the scientific world of the USSR. Two other contemporaries of Lamarck, Darwin and Mendel, also created "isms" and sparked the evolving science of genetics.

Charles Robert Darwin (1809-1882), rejected by medical school, became first a clergyman and then a travelling scientist. His interest in the population struggle and the results of inbreeding was aroused more by the writings of Malthus than by his own marriage to a first cousin. In his *Origin of Species* (1859), the process of natural selection as an expression of the struggle for survival was for the first time portrayed as the overriding principle responsible for the emergence of a new species. Each new species is a gamble, a novel "experiment," which is either doomed to failure and extinction (lethal mutant) or promoted to temporary success by the unique mutation. Darwinism is not only based on Lamarck's idea of linear evolution but also contains the dynamic principle between the organism and its adaptation to an often hostile milieu. It is also a stepping-stone to Mendelism.

Gregor Johann Mendel (1822-1884), the Czech-Austrian monk who without question has exerted the most remarkable influence on modern medical genetics, remained, during his lifetime, much less of a celebrity than Darwin. Mendel wished to become a biology teacher but never succeeded in passing his licensing examination. In the yard of the monastery where he lived, he began to experiment and to explore the regularities by which the generation-to-generation transmission of certain characteristics of the garden pea occurred. His experimentations began long before Darwin's first book was published, and they led to the eventual discovery of the basic laws of heredity. His disciplined and meticulous study of the tallness or dwarfness of these plants and the color of their flowers led Mendel to conclude the exact predictable proportion of the dominant and recessive features likely to occur in the next generation. Similar to many other characteristics, the tallness or shortness of each of these plants is determined by two factors, each provided by one parent. For example if both factors corresponded with the tall variety, the plant was a homozygote; if the two differed, it was a heterozygote. By means of self-pollination, that is, inbreeding, a 3:1 distribution between the ratio of the tall to the short varieties emerged in the heterozygous first generation, and a 1:2:1 distribution between the dominant and recessive characteristics was evident in the second generation. Such a mathematical predictability invariably signifies the proximity of a scientific principle. Despite the epochal significance of Mendel's discoveries and their publication in 1866, their enormous scientific value remained unrecognized for thirty-four years, only then to be suddenly, almost simultaneously, appreciated by three different scientists. Although the word *gene* dates from Wilhelm W. Johannsen in 1909, essentially it was Mendel who first described these units of hereditary transmission.

Each cell, except the normal circulating red blood cell, contains a nucleus. Inside the nucleus is a dark filament, named *chromosomes* by Walter Flemming and Anton Schneider in 1873. Not until fifteen years later were chromosomes noted by Waldeyer-Hartz as the substance responsible for cell division. Finally, in 1903, Sutton and Boveri recognized chromosomes as the cellular substance involved in hereditary transmission.

The number of chromosomes is a fixed characteristic in each species and never changes during the lifetime of a member of that species. In 1956, Tijo and Levan proved that the exact number of these protein-covered chromosomes in the normal human is 46. Of this number, 44 chromosomes are autosomes,

engaged in the role of carrying diverse traits, and two are sex
chromosomes, responsible, among other roles, for the determination of the sexual belonging of the individual. The bodies of
the chromosomes accommodate the innumerable large, molecule-
sized genes. The sex chromosomes are of two kinds: X and Y
chromosomes. Normally, although there are many potential
genetic pathologies, the 46XX constellation represents the human
female characteristics and the 46XY variety represents those
of the human male. The presence of a Y chromosome, apart
from rare abnormality, determines the maleness of the offspring.

Chromosomes in human male cells are present in pairs, i.e.
in diploid form. Before the two sex cells (the female ova, or
oocyte, and the male sperm cell, or spermatozoa) can unite,
they must undergo a cell division, meiosis, in which they lose
one-half of their chromosomes. They assume a haploid form so
that the union of the haploid male and female cells will again
yield 46 chromosomes, derived from both maternal and paternal
sources. There are artificial ways to circumvent this process.
J. B. Gurdon (1968) destroyed the nucleus of the female ovum
of the frog with ultraviolet radiation and replaced it with the
cell nucleus isolated from the intestinal cell of another frog, a
process known as cloning. By means of cloning the ovum was
"fertilized" and given a full set of chromosomes, all derived from
a single animal. The resulting offspring possessed the exclusive
characteristics of the frog that had provided the nucleus. Each
cell's chromosomes (and genes), regardless of their location in
the body, carry all the characteristics of the individual. Cloning
has been performed successfully in small animals. Theoretically,
cloning in the human is a feasible procedure. However, the
alleged human clone in David Rorvick's book (1978) is controversial and more than doubtful. The assembly of chromosomes
in a tissue or in white blood cells can be demonstrated by a
routine procedure that involves chemical stimulation followed
by chemical inhibition of cell division, and subsequent photog-
raphy under the microscope. A more recent technique, karyotyping, consists of cell exposure to a radioactive chemical, which
is then absorbed by the various chromosomes in varying degrees.
Because of their radioactivity, the chromosomes "photograph
themselves" when laid upon photographic film.

Numerical abnormality in both sex chromosomes and autosomes is well known. Such abnormality is frequently fatal in the autosomes in particular and usually has grave consequences in the sex chromosomes. Autosomal abnormality is frequently found in the tissues of miscarried fetuses; prenatal genetic diagnosis (Mennuti, 1977) of similar conditions is now feasible. The most common numerical chromosome abnormality is the superfluous number—trisomy—of the twenty-first pair of chromosomes, resulting in a form of mental retardation with physical stigmata known as Down's syndrome. Previously, this disorder was found more frequently in the children of older mothers. Recent data (Holmes, 1978), however, suggest that there is a decrease in the age of mothers transmitting this disorder. Also, the father may be the source of an extra twenty-first chromosome. Usually the abnormality is the result of a nondisjunction, that is, a failure of the split-up chromosome to unite in the meiotic phase of cell division.

In essence, chromosomes are mere vehicles for the conglomerates of large numbers of genes. The genes, with a prearranged "seat assignment," occupy a distinct position, a locus, on the chromosomes. Since chromosome pairs break up longitudinally and their number is halved during meiosis in both the male and female cells, a new combination of genes becomes possible through exchange of the loci upon union in the process of conception. T. H. Morgan and others have produced a linkage map of genes observing a simple and rapidly procreating organism, the drosophila, or sand fly. The drosophila, with its 4 chromosomes and 100 genes, produces some two dozen generations per year, making such a study feasible. Since the estimated number of genes in the mammalian species is 50 to 100×10^3 (Ohno, 1976), a similar linkage map of human genes is very complex and involves the careful study of marker genes. However, only meager results are available to date.

Male sexual development requires the presence of the Y chromosome. The lower portion of the long arm of the Y chromosome is recognizable by its fluorescent quality under the microscope. The nonfluorescent portion (Simpson, 1976) contains the male determining gene, which produces a substance, the H-Y antigen (Wachtel, Ohno and Koo, 1975). This H-Y antigen, by current knowledge, determines maleness by acting on the indifferent gonad and diverting its inherent propensity to develop into the basic sex, which is always female. Under the influence of this substance, a fetal testis develops in the male. The fetal testis will then produce two hormones (Ohno, 1976), the factor X, known from the research of Jost, and testosterone. The combined results of these two fetal substances is the prevention of female development and the induction of male evolvement. Sex determination, however, in its ultimate sense, directly or indirectly, involves thousands of genes that are hierarchically controlled (Ohno, 1976).

Among these thousands of genes engaged in shaping normal sexual development are many that are responsible for the normal evolvement of the internal and external genitalia, the step-by-step enzymatic chains in sex hormone production and the degree of sensitivity of the specific hormone receptors, which ultimately make the tissues responsive to the sex hormone effects. Each of these thousands of steps relates to known and to still unknown pathologies. For instance, the absence of one single specific X-linked gene determines an unresponsiveness of the tissues to testostereone derivates. A person lacking this particular gene, although chromosomally male, 46XY karyotype and possessing high levels of testosterone, will nevertheless develop into an externally unmistakable female, usually with very attractive female breasts, clitoris and a blind vagina, having frequent "inguinal hernias" that hide testes within. Such a condition can occur in complete and incomplete forms and is known as the testicular feminization syndrome, the essence of the disorder being an inability of the tissues to respond to testosterone.

It was stated that the presence of a Y chromosome is absolutely necessary for the normal male development, and indeed usually this is the case. Nevertheless, there are rare instances of 46XX males. The most frequent cause of this variation is a translocation of the masculinizing portion of the Y chromosome onto an X chromosome.

Some of the most common chromosomal disorders are those that affect the sex chromosomes (Gerald, 1976) and occur at the rate of 1:1100 females and 1:380 males. Park emphasizes that the effect of these chromosomal abnormalities upon the appearance and phenotype of the individual ranges from the subtle to the very pronounced.

Such a numerical chromosomal abnormality exists in Klinefelter's syndrome where a male karyotype of 47 XXY, that is, one with a feminine tinge, can be observed. Although phenotypically (in appearance) these individuals are unmistakably males, they show sterility and have small testes, low testosterone levels with elevated FSH and LH levels, and eunochoid, effeminate builds. Psychological, sexual and homosexual problems of various kinds are often evident. The frequency of this disorder is approximately 1:600 births (Gerald, 1976).

Another numerical chromosomal abnormality is gonadal dysgenesis, often referred to as Turner's syndrome. Persons with this disorder show an insufficient number of chromosomes: 45X. These individuals develop into females but are infertile, have amenorrhea, short stature, short, webbed necks and other physical stigmata, including characteristic fingerprints. They are usually very feminine in their psychological makeup. Should they adopt children, they are excellent mothers. No cases of Turner's syndrome have been reported to be lesbians. The disorder occurs in approximately 1:3000 females (Gerald, 1976) and is mostly transmitted paternally.

Both of the aforementioned conditions, as in other genetic or hormonal disorders, have numerous clinical variations and incomplete forms, and they exist in varying degrees—a situation that makes their detection difficult in routine examinations. Clinical evidence reported by Ionescu, Maxmilian and Bucur (1971) indicates that individuals who had experienced lifelong dissatisfaction with their respective genders were eventually found to have genetic abnormality, which, in the opinion of some authors, contributed to or determined the patients' displeasure concerning their original sex assignments. Similar instances described in the medical literature include patients with underdeveloped gonads (Benjamin, 1966), patients with estrogen-secreting testicular tumors (Stoller, 1960), patients with a feminizing suprarenal tumor (Routier, 1964), and individuals demonstrating Klinefelter's syndrome with transsexuality

(Brown, 1964; Davidson, 1966; Klotz, 1955; Money, 1967; Pauly, 1965).

Despite the spectacular advancement of medical genetics, much of the nature of genes remains unknown. Genes consist of the giant molecule deoxyribonucleic acid, or DNA. This complex and variable molecule with its mysterious inherent urge to replicate itself unless such replication is actively suppressed, stays inside the "sanctuary" of the cell nucleus. Other substances present there, the histones, repress the undue tendency of the DNA to replicate, thus preventing the formation of malignant tumors. The "recluse" DNA molecule communicates (transcribes) its "secret," the genetic code, only to another cousin substance, ribonucleic acid, or RNA. The RNA then carries this message further and translates this information to the protein-producing part of the cell, the ribosome. The complex process was first described by Watson and Crick. The genetic code, consisting of a particular and infinitely variable sequence of amino acids was deciphered by Nirenberg and Matthei in 1961. Finally, in the same year, the intricate system of genes and their controlling, supervising and regulating of all protein, peptide and enzyme production of the body was proposed by Jacob and Monod.

Genes provide a vast assortment of information, and their emitted chemical signals determine characteristics from the color of the eye to the blood group. Many of the genes begin their activity only at a later specific time during the life span of the individual and thus bring to manifestation various conditions that did not previously exist. Apart from some specific states described above, no genes are known to definitely determine sexual choice or preference at large. If and when such information emerges at a future time, it will likely be found in the genes rather than in the chromosomes. Even though such genetic information is not available to date, a strong denial of such a possibility in favor of other unproven hypotheses would be unwise.

Under certain conditions, male and female cells can be recognized by means of ordinary microscopic examination. M. L. Barr found typical, dark-stained, small round structures located peripherally within the nuclei of the cells of the normal female. They are best detected in certain periods of cell division (interphase). For investigation, a light scraping from the mouth or cervix provides cells that are easily detected after staining. They are commonly referred to as Barr bodies or sex chromatin, although more precisely they should be called X-sex chromatin. These bodies actually represent an immobilized X chromosome. M. F. Lyon (1961) found that all except one X chromosome in a cell will be inactivated and will form sex chromatin bodies. Since the female contains two X chromosomes and the male one, the inactivation of the "superfluous" X chromosome in the female offspring begins in the earliest period of life after conception; thus, the sex of a fetus can be determined from a sample of the amniotic fluid obtained from the pregnant mother. A chromosomally normal female will have one Barr body and a male none. A female with Turner's syndrome, having only a single X chromosome, will have no Barr bodies; whereas a male with Klinefelter's syndrome, possessing two X chromosomes, will have one, just like the normal female. This procedure permits the determination of nuclear sex, a method less reliable (because of these exceptions) than karyotyping. Recently an F-sex chromatin was shown in the cells of the male, consisting of the fluorescent part of the Y chromosome.

Polani (1970) demonstrated that some fragments of the inactivated X chromosomes retain some activity or are even reactivated at a later point in life for some unknown reason. Since female traits are attached to the X chromosome, which is the one that may undergo reactivation, one wonders about the significance of such chromosomal restoration, particularly in clinical cases of late manifestation of transsexualism or other sexual disorders. To the author's knowledge, no such investigations have yet been made; therefore, one must wait before drawing conclusions.

Nevertheless, genetically determined degrees of psychological and behavioral maleness and femaleness can be laid out on a longitudinal line. It is not the normal female who is the most feminine, nor the normal male who is the most masculine. The highest degree of psychological femininity would be shown in a case of Turner's syndrome, followed by a 46XY male with high testosterone levels having a testicular feminization syndrome, both being more feminine than the normal female. Then, at the masculine end of the scale, a case of Klinefelter's syndrome would be followed by a female with an adrenocortical masculinization syndrome, both being less masculine than the normal male. Recently two instances of transsexuality were reported by Buhrich and co-workers (1978) in two male patients with 47XYY constellation, a chromosomal condition regarded by some as "supermale."

CHAPTER 5

CLINICAL ASPECTS OF TRANSSEXUALITY

Unless so urged as teenagers by distraught parents, transsexuals are almost always motivated to see a psychiatrist driven by a fervent desire to obtain a recommendation for transsexual surgery. This is probably the reason why some psychiatrists (Van Putten, 1976; Knorr, 1968) observed that the life histories provided by these patients are likely to be biased and seem to have a conspicuously stereotypic flavor. Rightly so in some instances, but mistakenly in many others, such patients are often accused of "telling what the psychiatrist needs to hear" for purposes of attaining their goal. Encountering this opinion, it should be considered that every medical or psychopathological entity, be it diabetes or schizophrenia, has a group of commonly shared features, and that it is precisely this stereotyping that provides the necessary profile of the disorder and renders it diagnostically recognizable. Such too is the case with transsexualism.

The abovementioned authors have highlighted, in particular, the striking similarity in the developmental history of male transsexuals. Indeed, the sequence of their life events contains a multitude of recurring elements: showing an early childhood inclination to play with female toys, having "typical" feminine inclinations and an urge to relate to female playmates, experiencing admiration and craving for female clothes, with episodic crossdressing and sexual-emotional attraction to boys, and revealing an identification with the female role.

The beginning of these feelings and tendencies is lost in the hazy memory of infancy. Later, usually from puberty onward, a growing dissatisfaction with their male anatomy becomes apparent and is accompanied by exclusive or almost exclusive sexual outlet with men. These phenomena represent the characteristic milestones of the disorder. Knorr (1968), in concordance with Money (1969) and Guze (1966-67), recognizes that gender identity disorders antedate genital sexuality and the early imprinting of core gender identity previously mentioned. Transsexuals are viewed with skepticism in professional circles, and a "Catch-22" often lingers on when they are being evaluated by gender clinics: their story is either "too good," and raises the suspicion of distortion of their life events, or it is "not typical" and results in a hunt for other diagnostic labels.

The truth is that many transsexuals will give a more-or-less "typical" past life story while many others will not. In the latter category can be classified instances that the author refers to as the "late manifestation cases."

An abridged history of some emblematic cases may prove helpful.

Patient 1

This is the case of a twenty-three-year-old, single, attractive "female" nightclub entertainer who presented herself in such tasteful, feminine attire that no one suspected that "she" was an anatomical male. The patient had already had breast implants and had used female hormones regularly. She had dressed, lived and worked exclusively as a female for three years with a begrudging, then supporting approval from her parents. Her femininity was convincing and casual without being exaggerated. She had a fiancé and many girlfriends with whom she enjoyed "girl talk." She liked wearing fashionable slacks, had a décolleté and wore some jewelry on her well-manicured hands (Figs. 5-1 and 5-2). Self-assured and intelligent, she had no discomfort whatever. The single purpose of her visit was to gain support for her transsexual surgery. She needed only minimal facial electrolysis, as she had practically no facial hair growth. An earlier endocrine workup demonstrated the isolated deficiency of the pituitary FSH hormone; a testicular biopsy indicated atrophy of the seminiferous tubules; and she showed some hyperosmia. Sexually, she related exclusively to men. Her sexual gratification resulted not so much from her own orgasm as from "having fulfilled the role of the female" and having provided satisfaction to her partner. The patient's mother, a colorful, feminine, "open-minded" person was always close to the patient, while the father, a disabled laborer, was somewhat distant. There was no history of psychiatric illness in the family. The results of a full psychological testing were evaluated by two independent psychologists, one of whom was unaware of the patient's problem. Some egocentricity and narcissism were present; one of the psychologists suspected some personality disorder. All other psychiatric and physical examinations were normal, except for the mild hypothalamopituitary problem of FSH levels.

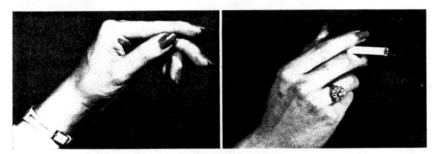

Figure 5-1. Feminine hands of the transsexual male.

Drawn to "girlish" styles of play and the company of girlfriends from the earliest age on, this patient became a member of a dance group around ten years of age and had repeated successful appearances on television, occasionally while dressed as a girl. Earlier crossdressing had also taken place. From puberty on, crossdressing became increasingly frequent, the practice making her "feel natural," with no sexual component. After the awakening of her sexual interest, the patient's attraction was exclusively male directed. Her sexual partners were male homosexuals "out of necessity, not preference," as she craved the love of the unattainable "real man." Surgery was performed on this patient; subsequent surgical repair rendered the artificial vagina functional (Figs. 5-3 and 5-4). For three years as of this writing, the patient has been extremely happy and well adjusted.

Both the physical and the psychological factors being

simultaneously operant in this patient's case, an opportunity to speculate as to their etiology arises. Neither the physical nor the psychological factors explain her transsexualism satisfactorily. The permissive, possibly subtly encouraging mother, not unlike Stoller's description, was present in the patient's life as a guiding object, as were the learned experiences of reinforcing successes within the feminine role. A hypothalamopituitary hormonal dysfunction represents the biological influence.

Patient 2

This is the case of a twenty-four-year-old "barmaid" whom no one suspected of being male. She lived common-law with a divorced nonhomosexual male and used to work as a strip-teaser but disliked this because she found it "vulgar." Since the age of six she had lived in a "world of girlfriends" and played with dolls. An attractive and kind mother confessed that she had always wanted a girl, even though the patient was the second of two boys and four girls. During her pregnancy with the patient the mother underwent some kind of "female hormone treatment." The father was distant, had some alcoholic problems, and often accused the patient's mother of "bringing him up to be a homosexual." The patient had her first sexual relations at fourteen years of age with a man; she had never had sexual relations with a female. The only physical signs of her maleness were scanty hair growth, rarely requiring shaving, and a flat five-hour glucose tolerance curve, indicating possible hypothalamic sluggishness. The patient adapted excellently to surgery.

Patient 3

This twenty-three-year-old hairdresser and former "waitress" lived as a woman for years in a common-law relationship with a divorced man who "never was homosexual." She had previously had a similar relationship with another man. The patient was obese but attractive, with scanty facial hair and an absence of body hair. She was the oldest in a poor family of six children, one of whom was a boy and the rest girls. Her childhood history was chaotic because of her father's alcoholism and brutality. The patient had bright intelligence and female identity, and she had crossdressed since childhood. She had never had sex with a female. Physical abnormalities included the absence of body hair and scanty facial hair. In addition, Barr bodies were found in the buccal smear on three subsequent occasions, indicating the presence of female cells in spite of the fact that karyotyping was that of the male pattern. She adapted excellently to surgery despite physical complications that resulted in repeated surgeries and urinary difficulties.

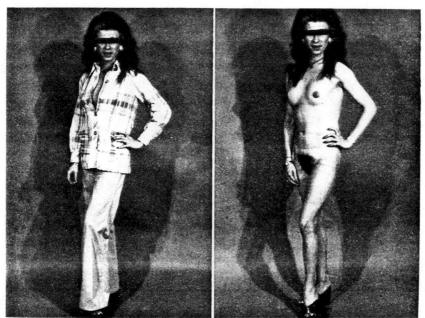

Figure 5-2. Before transsexual surgery.

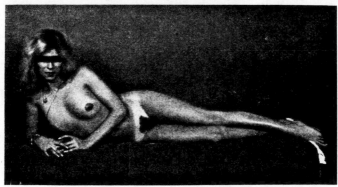

Figure 5-3. After transsexual surgery.

Just as women have different styles of conduct, personality, ambition and class, so do transsexuals. Some are ostentatious and seductive, while others are refined, shy and modest. Commonly shared among them, though, are the developmental events of their lives and the problems arising from them, problems infinitely more complex and painful than those of homosexuals. Many of these features are well portrayed in the autobiographies of some transsexuals, such as that of Canary Conn.

Among the many transsexual histories the author has gathered is one very impressive case of a young, very poorly educated man from an economically and culturally deprived family in a small rural district. Neither the patient nor his family had ever even heard about transsexualism. Nonetheless, he has passed through all the typical transsexual developmental phases, the earliest of which went as far back in his past as his memory could reach. Isolated from all external information and possessed by his inner overpowering urges, he was puzzled and horrified as he submitted to his incomprehensible drive to cross-dress. At puberty he developed an increasing dislike for his male anatomy and craved men sexually. He thought he was the only creature in the world with these peculiar sensations. He came to the conclusion that he was a homosexual, but the scattered homosexual experiences he had soon convinced him otherwise. He could not account for his drives and thought he must be crazy. He had become depressed and had made a suicide attempt resulting in psychiatric hospitalization when he was referred to the author. He had not heard of the famous case of Christine Jorgensen and had never before met a transsexual. It was amazing to observe his relief when he was first exposed to such company; he soon made a good adaptation with hormone treatment. He now lives, dresses and works as a woman and awaits surgery with an unwavering desire.

This leads us to a seldom-discussed aspect of the clinical evaluation of patients for transsexual surgery. A candidate for such surgery, if pretty and feminine in the popular sense of the word, with a small body frame and winning personality features, is more likely to receive the verdict so important to "her." Another candidate, lacking these characteristics, is often rejected, not because "she" is not "as feminine" as the other but because the examiner cannot visualize such a person in the female role. In some places (Yardley, 1976) feminine skills are taught to male transsexuals as a preoperative procedure. The rationale is that once a patient has decided on transsexual surgery and the gender team supports this decision, the patient might as well be apt in the chosen role.

Masculine features are common among transsexuals except for heavy body hair, although such can be observed among homosexuals and fetishistic transvestites.

It is commonly agreed that psychotic patients, sociopaths and mentally retarded individuals are unsuitable candidates for transsexual surgery. These warnings are not always heeded by all. The author saw an unfortunate patient suffering from paranoid schizophrenia on whom the first stage in a two-stage type of surgery was performed. As expected, his adaptation to the new sexual role was poor. This example should not be confused with those instances where surgery with "unease" (Stoller, 1973) was performed on insistent, but not quite suitable, candidates. Stoller describes such cases, but investigation of the literature shows that many similar ones were included in almost all other series. Thus, instances of frank psychotics (Stoller, 1973), men well over fifty years of age at the time of surgery, one with a previous leucotomy (Hoenig, 1971), without any genuine desire to be female (Van Putten, 1976), had sex-change operations with poor results. One man, well into his fifties when the surgery took place, demanded to be "changed back" at the age of sixty-four years. Another patient, in whom the possibility of a paroxysmal disorder does not appear to have been excluded, was actually "changed back" with mastectomy and hormone treatment (Money, 1973).

Another difficulty lies with those cases that have atypical transsexual histories. There are many in this category who had abundant heterosexual relations in the past or who even married and fathered children. The oldest the author has encountered in this group was a fifty-four-year-old divorced father of two children. He reputedly had a "pituitary problem" in infancy and was growing at a slow rate. He had a single experience of crossdressing in his childhood. Between fourteen and eighteen years of age, he had some bisexual experiences and a "significant" homosexual experience at eighteen years. Subsequently, he joined the Army and got married when he was discharged. He had no homosexual experiences after eighteen years of age. His sexual relations, although described as "low keyed," were mutually satisfactory, as were the other aspects of his marriage. In his mid-forties, the temptation to crossdress emerged. He increasingly gave in to these urges, began to have homosexual fantasies, and felt good in female company. Finally, he confessed his need to "become a female" to his wife. In a very civilized manner, the couple divorced, and for the last six years he has lived, dressed and worked as a female. Since then he has had some homosexual relationships, providing him with the satisfaction of "feeling feminine." He is taking female hormones and is considered as a good candidate for transsexual surgery.

In late-manifestation cases, one has to consider the possibility that many distinctly genetically determined illnesses may appear clinically at a later stage in life. We are still far from being able to provide an ultimate answer as to how and why transsexualism may appear at a later stage of life. In this regard, one has to consider a number of psychological and some biological factors. Psychologically, the possibility of an underlying weakness of the gender identity can be safely assumed. Physically, conditions that reduce or even extinguish sexual potency can often, but not always be, demonstrated. One such condition is diabetes mellitus. A sizeable portion of the diabetic male population suffers from impotence. This, of course, does not mean that a person rendered impotent by diabetes will invariably become transsexual or manifest other sexual anomalies. On the other hand, however, the author found a higher rate of diabetes and diabetic relatives in the transsexual population. Whether or not a physical impediment to the potency of a person contributes significantly to the derailment of his/her sexuality can be neither firmly established nor disregarded.

In at least one instance, the author encountered a situation where diabetes could be regarded as a decisive factor in bringing about transsexualism. This was the case of a transsexual man in his mid-twenties who had suffered from a brittle, insulin-dependent childhood diabetes since ten years of age. He also had diabetes-determined impotence all his life. Although diabetes can bring about impotence, it does not diminish the sexual drive. With the libido high and the potency impaired, it is understandable that the sexual outlet will be modified; unable to be "active," he still can be "passive," and thus "feminine," as far as male fantasy goes.

However, the significance of the potential physical factors will not be emphasized here beyond the point that can be proven to be valid by current understanding. The author merely wishes to state that these factors have not yet been explored sufficiently and that clinical assessments of transsexual patients in this regard are still grossly deficient.

In some clinical forms of transsexuality, one can find historical layers of life events that may be misleading in the accurate diagnosis of a patient and that illustrate once more the concept of the spectrum of varieties of sexual disorders. A clinical example will clarify this statement.

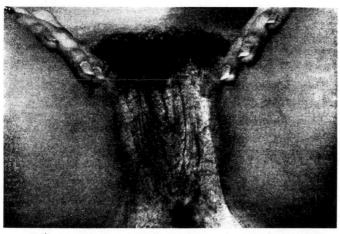

Figure 5-4. Artificial vagina with insufficient opening, requiring corrective surgery.

A "transsexual" man in his thirties, married and the father of two children, had been secretly crossdressing for many years. He enjoyed female clothing and felt a "satisfaction" when he indulged in this practice. He was not usually "turned on" sexually when he crossdressed, but when he occasionally was, he found an outlet with masturbation. He had never had homosexual relations. Thus, one might say that he was really a transvestite. Yet he had some homosexual fantasies and, above all, a desire to undergo transsexual surgery. His history revealed that from ten to fourteen years of age he shared a bedroom with his older sister. His sister often wore only panties and bra, and the patient, pretending to sleep, encouraged this practice. He often handled his sister's undergarments and experienced sexual arousal. Finally he slipped into the panties; even without arousal, "it felt good." So far this history reflects the course of transvestism. However, in his early childhood, he preferred to play with dolls, preferred the company of girls and crossdressed on a few occasions as early as two years of age. These practices are quite distinctly within the transsexual realm.

In similar cases, where the distinction between diagnostic labels becomes obliterated, the physician does best by disregarding them. More important is the study of the persistency of the patient's desire for sex change, his ego strength, his overall functioning and the reality factors operant in his life. The overriding significance of these factors and the absence of absolute or fixed criteria in regard to transsexual surgery were emphasized by Money and co-workers (Money, Hampson and Hampson, 1957). Thus, the physician is placed in the lonely and difficult position of undertaking a decision based on the individual study of each and every patient.

Ultimately, it is the element of time that usually provides the correct answer, along with the estrogen treatment of the patient. If a transsexual male patient with reasonably good ego can live, work and dress as a female, get estrogen treatment with consequential breast development and impotence, which are easily reversible consequences, in time (often one or two years), he will be regarded as a good candidate for the irreversible surgical procedure.

A word of warning should be passed on concerning men who "wish to be lesbians." Some men, who most frequently are transvestites and heterosexuals, may suffer from total or partial impotency. They may be part-time crossdressers; they may work as men but in their privacy or, as rarely happens, while living with a "butch" lesbian, may enjoy crossdressing. They savor a sense of femaleness, which they equate with the human qualities of being kind, good, sensitive and creative. Such men have formed various national and international "sisterhoods" of male-feminism, a harmless and, for them, pleasurable, although somewhat sexist, indulgence. They are rarely, if ever, motivated for psychotherapy, the effectiveness or even the purpose of which is questionable. They may, however, present themselves for transsexual surgery or estrogen treatment but are poor candidates for either.

The nature of the relationship and some of the preoperative and everyday problems of some transsexuals are very well portrayed in a (minimally) edited letter written to the author by a patient's fiancé:

Dear Dr. Koranyi:

Re: M
An Update (Oct. 20, 1978)

Permit me to re-introduce myself again. I am M's friend, and though we haven't met these many months since you made your final assessment of M, I thought it was time to update you on her.

First of all, I have glad tidings! By telephone tonight, M informs me that Dr. L is willing to perform the surgery. His operating schedule is presently tight, and he is unable to do it prior to December 7th. So, it looks like we are looking at a possible surgery date of mid-December and possibly as late as the early part of January. In any regard, she and I are delighted with this news from Toronto.

I often refer to these many past months starting when M first met you (March, 1977) as months of Agony and Exuberation. There were times when her nerves and mine were pushed to the limit as she adjusted to the effects of estrogen upon her nervous system. There are adjustments going on still, and undoubtedly they will continue to some lesser degree. Our relationship has been tested in many ways, and yet we still share that closeness and concern for one another. Neither she nor I know exactly what the next few months will bring, after the operation. I do know that M is happier than she has ever been in her life, and I foresee that it can only get better. She is, as you know, my dependent and I have tried to protect her throughout these months of change. She is gaining confidence in herself, taking an interest in pursuing some of her artistic talent in a career yet to be decided upon, either in modelling, dancing or hairstyling. I have told her that I will support these efforts with further financial backing if she wishes to take lessons. I am interested in seeing the lady function as normally as possible with a sense of independence and self-assuredness. I think you and I want this for her.

The Florida holiday we needed very badly. We were living so close to her problem and had built up such expectations when we had thought it was first possible for Dr. B to do the surgery in the early part of last February. We had to get away from a life built around doctors' appointments, and countdowns to surgery which ended only in disappointment.

On the holiday, for the entire month of August M's mother and married sister joined us for a stay at my parent's Florida home. My mother had passed away suddenly last March in Florida, and we assured my father that we would make the trip to dispose of my mother's personal effects, as well as look after matters left unfinished in his haste to return to Canada for funeral arrangements. This was a heavy burden on us all—both M and I and my father felt this loss greatly. However, we made the best of the situation and have been left a rich treasury of memories.

While on holiday, M found that men indeed were interested in her in a very flattering heterosexual way. This put a strain on our relationship, as I tried to come to understand why M needed time to sort her feelings out, and experience all this male attention denied to her throughout those formative years when young ladies (without her problem) are courted and wooed. In time, I understood that I would again have to be patient, supportive, and liberal in my approach. I had almost developed a motherly concern for M sensing a danger to her when heterosexual males "get turned on" to what they think is a very attractive and complete female. M can handle herself; has a good instinct as to how far their intentions may or may not be honourable (to speak in an old-fashioned sense) and when and how far she can presently operate with safety in this world of the interested male. To me, Doctor, it has been an education . . . an education in living, and an experience few can (nor perhaps wish to) have given equal circumstances.

M is presently in the good care of a friend J, enjoying her hospitality this weekend in Toronto. J is the young lady from Toronto whom you met in joint session with G and M when you were interested in discussing common problems of transsexuals. G introduced us to her . . . a close friendship has developed, and we are indeed grateful to J that M can stay with her during times of visits to Dr. L and the immediate post-operative period. Having gone through surgery 18 months ago, by the same Dr. L, she is in a unique position to help M with recovery and making the physical, medical adjustments.

On the financial side, I am given to understand that the operation itself will cost $950.00 with $225.00 for surgical assistance, and hospital charges of $192.00 per day for at least a ten day period. Fortunately, I have two-thirds of these expenses, and assurances from my father to meet the balance. I am given to understand that O.H.I.P. and Blue Cross coverage in this case will not apply, even though I have born the expense of PAY DIRECT schemes for M for semi-private and drug-prescriptions coverage (Blue Cross) since she left employment and started treatment. Added to this, M has started expensive electrolysis treatments for facial hair removal. To date $500.00 has been spent in upwards of three and one half hours per week since mid-September of extremely painful treatments. M is surviving this well, determined to bear the pain and have an end to bothersome and embarrassing hair growth in this noticeable area (so important to her well-being as a female).

On this note, I wonder if I might have a letter from you indicating that these treatments are for medical reasons, and NOT for cosmetic reasons. Also, indicate in this letter, if you will, that I have been her sole financial supporter and that you are knowledgeable about this. I will attempt to submit these expensive electrolysis receipts in my 1978 income tax declaration as medical expenses for a dependent.

I see that I have gone on here at considerable length, and wish to apologize for the involvement and detail undertaken in what was meant, at first, to be a letter of mere notification and good wishes.

I shall endeavour to keep you informed as best I can. I realize that you have a busy schedule, and little could be gained by personal contacts, in this post-assessment period from M.

W.P.

P.S.—The law firm of_____is presently in charge of M's application for a legal change of name. Ms. X will be approaching you after the operation for supporting medical affidavits to approach the Provincial Court on M's behalf. We are anxious to normalize her lifestyle as soon as possible, after the fact of the surgery.

CHAPTER 6

MEDICO-LEGAL ASPECTS OF HOMOSEXUALITY, TRANSVESTISM AND TRANSSEXUALITY AND LEGAL COMPLICATIONS SURROUNDING SEX REASSIGNMENT SURGERY

SELWYN M. SMITH AND BETTY J. LYNCH

INTRODUCTION

Elsewhere in this volume, definitions of the terms *homosexual, transvestite and transsexual* are supplied and differences between them are explained. Religious taboos had for centuries made these conditions in general, and homosexuality in particular, crimes that were "not fit to be named among Christian men" or "the very mention of which is a disgrace to human nature" (Crompton, 1976). Such attitudes severely inhibited legislative advancement and medical understanding of these phenomena. This chapter will trace some of the historical attitudes towards these conditions and present some of the practical legal dilemmas facing those who suffer from these abnormalities.

Among the ancient tribes of Israel, homosexuality was both practiced and condemned. Because homosexuality had ritualistic significance for alien religions, special force was lent to this condemnation. Genesis 19 contains the story of a group of debauched men of Sodom who stormed the house where Lot was, demanding, "Where are the men which came into thee this night? Bring them out to us so that we may know them." Lot offered his virgin daughters instead. A similar story appears in Judges 19. The history of David and Jonathan in the book of Samuel, whose love was "passing the love of women," and the story of the love of Ruth and Naomi (Ruth 1) have been cited as examples of homosexual romance (West, 1968).

Male homosexual sentiment permeated the whole fabric of Greek society. Homosexuality meant more to the Greeks than a safety valve for excess lust; it was in their eyes the highest and noblest of passions. They idealized the love of man for man as much as present-day Western civilization idealizes romantic love between man and woman. The Greeks, however, did not encourage indiscriminate infatuations. Socrates' fascination for youths brought him no credit. The cult of effeminacy in young men and the buying or selling of sexual favors evoked the strongest disapproval. The penal code of ancient Athens included various provisions against homosexual abuses, some of which dated from Solon's enactments in the sixth century B.C. Though relations between adult citizens were permitted, Solon forbade a slave to have association with a freeborn youth on pain of a public whipping. Legislation also provided for the removal of all civil rights from any Athenian citizen who prostituted his body for money. The legal code also took special care to protect children from seduction. For assault against a minor a man could be sentenced to death or to a heavy fine. A father (or guardian) who prostituted his son for gain was liable to severe punishment, as was the man who took advantage of the boy, although the boy himself, provided he was underage, suffered no legal penalty.

Nineteenth century England was replete with scandals. Foreign Minister Castlereagh committed suicide out of a fear, probably delusional, of being denounced. Oscar Wilde was imprisoned following three sensational trials and was convicted largely on the evidence of self-confessed male prostitutes and blackmailers who turned Queen's evidence and accordingly went free. The learned judge expressed his utmost indignation at the evidence of corruption of the most hideous kind and regretted that the maximum penalty he was allowed to give Oscar Wilde was totally inadequate. A sobering comment by the writer W. T. Stead describes an opposing viewpoint: "Should everyone found guilty of Oscar Wilde's crime be imprisoned, there would be a very surprising emigration from Eton, Harrow, Rugby and

Winchester, to the gaols of Pentonville and Holloway (West, 1968).

LAWS AGAINST HOMOSEXUALITY, TRANSVESTISM AND TRANSSEXUALITY

In the thirteenth century, homosexuality was generally regarded as a "clerical vice" (Goodich, 1976). Up until the thirteenth century, the vices were generally dealt with in the manuals of penance, which regulated the penalties to be imposed by the clergy upon their erring flocks. Both secular and church legislation made extensive use of scriptural remarks dealing with homosexuality that were largely found in the Old Testament. These important references concerned the fate of Sodom and Gomorrah and suggested death by conflagration as the proper punishment for sodomites (Genesis 13-19). This is reiterated by the legal code found in Leviticus 18:22. The Old Testament prescribed the death penalty for male homosexuality but made no reference to lesbianism. However, church canonists interpreting the traditions of Roman law as they bore on sodomy regularly included lesbian acts as meriting capital punishment, and records exist of executions in France and Italy (Crompton, 1976).

It is remarkable that this phraseology remained on the books of at least one American state—Connecticut—until some forty-six years after the Declaration of Independence. In the early part of the thirteenth century, homosexuality was equated with homicide in its seriousness as a sin against God's law and a contradiction of the divine injunction to increase and multiply. The grim saga of homosexuals in colonial America has been reviewed in detail by Crompton (1976).

The influence of Quaker humanitarianism in Pennsylvania, however, promulgated laws that were landmarks in Christian legislation. Because of the Quakers' aversion to the shedding of blood, this new code limited the death penalty to cases of murder and, for the first time, introduced prison sentences for other crimes. Penalty for homosexual acts was reduced to six months imprisonment, a lesser penalty than any American state would adopt until 1961. Pennsylvania's Quaker Code provided that "if any person shall be Legally Convicted of the unnatural sin of Sodomy or joining with beasts, Such persons shall be whipt and forfeit one-third of his or her estate, and work six months in the House of Correction at hard labor, and for the Second offence, imprisonment as aforesaid, during life (Staughton et al., 1879).

In a similar vein, transvestism, although considered a sin against God, was not openly recognized or penalized to the extent that homosexuality was. Deuteronomy 22:5 states that "no woman shall wear an article of man's clothing, nor shall man put on a woman's dress, for those who do these things are abominable to the Lord, your God." Though transvestism was condemned, there was no mention of penalties to be enacted. This may reflect the fact that transvestism was not viewed as coming within the orbit of the sodomy statutes. Transvestism was a practice that was engaged in privately out of a fear of retribution from family and friends.

In contrast to homosexuality, there is no explicit mention in historical writings of transsexualism or societal sanctions against such behavior. It is possible that this paucity of documentation may be due to the absence of sufficient knowledge in medicine, law and science in dealing with such a disorder. A transsexual desiring a gender change centuries ago was most likely to be considered a homosexual, but no resources were available to deal with the subject of gender identity confusion. Such individuals would most probably be persecuted under the sodomy statutes for deviant sexual activity.

The above review highlights the fact that sanctions against sexual deviants were enacted mostly in an effort to appease God and also to maintain a certain genetic purity. Such attitudes undoubtedly influenced current legislation and continue to create problems for those afflicted by these abnormalities.

SOME LEGAL PROBLEMS

Homosexuality

In many civilized countries, homosexual behavior does not contravene the law except in special circumstances of abuse, for instance if children are involved or when force is used to coerce an unwilling participant. In other places, e.g. in most parts of North America, including Canada, any kind of sexual contact between persons of the same sex is regarded as a serious crime. The peculiar legal terminology referring to such offenses as "crimes against nature," "immoral conduct" and "acts of indecency" prudishly avoid spelling out the details of the offenses in question and allows the judiciary a considerable degree of latitude in interpreting the law. In certain situations where the laws may appear to be extremely harsh, homosexuals may in fact be allowed to live in comparative tranquility, free from prosecution or harrassment by police and civic authorities. In the East and in the Arab world, male homosexual behavior arouses little public concern, and even the presence of male brothels is treated with indifference or amusement, despite the fact that very serious religious or legal crimes are being committed. However, in 1966 in Yemen, a Moslem religious court convicted a sixty-year-old government worker of pederasty and sentenced him to death.

The laws governing sex conduct have been derived, as mentioned above, from ancient religious codes. The Christian church adopted the ancient Jewish sex codes and formalized them into the ecclesiastical laws that governed medieval Europe and later provided the basis for English common law. As late as the eighteenth century homosexuals were burnt at the stake in Paris. Liberal change emerged in the sex laws in Europe following the French Revolution of 1789. Later systematized and widely promulgated in the Napoleonic Code of 1810, this philosophy still provides the basis for sex legislation of many European countries. In recent decades, French law has been slightly altered so as to discriminate against homosexual activity. Relations with a consenting teenager of the opposite sex are permitted, in contrast to a penalty of from ten months to three years imprisonment, plus a fine, for those who indulge in any indecent or unnatural act with someone of the same sex aged under twenty-one. Public indecency is more severely punished if the behavior is homosexual rather than heterosexual. Prostitution, either heterosexual or homosexual, does not in itself constitute an offense against French law, although importuning for immoral purposes carries a penalty of several days imprisonment. The age of legal consent has been set at twenty-one in France and Holland but is somewhat lower in Denmark, Sweden, Greece, Italy, Norway and Switzerland.

The 1926 Penal Code of postrevolutionary Russia made no reference to homosexuality, but since that time the law has become more stringent. In 1934 a Soviet decree was issued that made sex acts between males an offense. Homosexuality was designated a "social crime" and equated with sabotage, espionage and counterrevolutionary activity. It was punishable in lighter cases by three to five years imprisonment. Homosexuality also remains a crime in both East and West Germany. In 1935, under the Nazi regime, penalties were considerably increased and all types of indecent acts were punishable.

American legislation controlling sexual behavior varies from state to state. Plain copulation between husband and wife is the only sexual act that is not regarded as a crime in any state. Other forms of marital foreplay, solitary masturbation and premarital or adulterous sexual behavior are all crimes in one state or another. Antihomosexual attitudes are backed by public opinion, resulting in the fact that technically many heterosexual Americans are criminals.

Although state legislatures are increasingly considering legal reforms that will remove criminal penalties from homosexual activities in private between consenting adults, the great majority of American jurisdictions nevertheless continue to outlaw any type of homosexual act whether consensual or not. Response for legal reform has emerged with the growing demands of the minorities for full legal rights. There has also been a general breakdown in the conspiracy of silence that has traditionally surrounded homosexuality (Geis, 1976). Considerable controversy continues to exist concerning the possible impact of altering legislation. Controversy surrounds the question of whether decriminalization will encourage homosexual behavior and/or increase its visibility. There is also concern with the effect that decriminalization might have on other forms of criminal behavior and upon law enforcement procedures. Every state in the union, except Illinois, makes some or all homosexual acts a criminal offense, even when carried out between consenting adults in private. Felony statutes mostly refer to "sodomy" or "crimes against nature," for which the maximum penalty in several states is life imprisonment and in other states over ten years of imprisonment. North Carolina has a minimum punishment of five years imprisonment.

Misdemeanor statutes covering acts "outrageous to public decency" can be used for controlling male importuning or loitering around public lavatories, while homosexual conduct in private may be prosecuted as "lewd," "obscene" or "indecent" behavior. Since many of the statutes apply equally to heterosexual and homosexual activity, erotic bedroom activities that were once a source of pleasure to both husband and wife may suddenly become grounds for a charge of cruelty or for unfitness to have custody of children. Disastrous consequences to all members of the family, especially the children, have occurred as a result of intimate details appearing in newspaper articles. Homosexuals may also be liable to prosecution as vagrants, that is to say, "lewd, disorderly or dissolute persons." Such ambiguous definitions make possible the arrest of homosexuals whose conversation, mannerism or style of dress appear objectionable to the police, even though they may not have been indulging in any illicit sexual act.

Legal problems have been compounded for homosexuals by the fact that during the past three decades more than half the states have enacted sexual-psychopath legislation. There are also civil commitment procedures in all states applicable to the mentally ill who might constitute a "danger to themselves or others" and who are "in need of care or treatment." There is no uniformity in the definition of the sexual psychopath or in the circumstances that call for initiation of special proceedings. In general the term *sexual psychopath* is defined as "one lacking the power to control his sexual impulses or having criminal propensities towards the commission of sex offenses" (Slovenko, 1973). The law has taken the position of dealing with the status of being rather than actual doing. Enforcement of the sexual psychopath law has therefore resulted in a roundup of the vagrant and nuisance type of offender and has failed to reach the dangerous or aggressive offender. Special institutions, such as the Atascadero State Hospital in California, have been created to implement the sexual psychopath legislation. Such institutions have been generally regarded as failures. Special institutions for the sexual psychopath, like special institutions for persons deemed incompetent to stand trial, are not justified (Slovenko, 1973).

Sexual psychopath legislation does no more than detain individuals who are regarded as freaks, apply a stigmatization and then render them forever social outcasts. The Goodrich Act of 1935 is a perfect example of how legislation appears in an effort to allay public hysteria arising from the commission of brutal crimes by an individual. This futile legislation was repealed in 1968.

More recently, the model penal code prepared by the American Law Institute has been prominent in suggesting that private sexual acts of a heterosexual or homosexual nature should be criminal only where minors are involved or some force or coercion is used. Since 1962 this reform has been put into effect in Illinois and several other states. Decriminalization of homosexuality, however, will not provide a panacea. Wilson and Chappell (1968) reported no change in the incidence of homosexuality following its decriminalization in Holland. Similarly, reports regarding the pioneer efforts of the 1962 Illinois decriminalization statute maintained that it has been ineffective in providing protection for homosexuals.

Hoffman (1969) reported that homosexuals in Chicago experienced more difficulties with the law following enactment of the new penal code compared with homosexuals in other parts of the United States. Gunnison (1969) has suggested that removal of sodomy from the Illinois code has caused the police to become more intense in their pursuit of homosexuals under the solicitation laws of the state.

In England, homosexual crimes first became a matter for the secular courts in 1533, when a statute was introduced making sodomy punishable by death. This remained in force until the nineteenth century, when the maximum penalty was reduced to life imprisonment. The Offences Against the Persons Act, 1861, Section 61, which remained in .force until 1956, stated, "Whoever shall be convicted of the Abominable Crime of Buggery committed with mankind or any animal shall be liable at the discretion of the court, to imprisonment for life." Under the criminal law amendment act of 1885, all sexual acts between males of any age became offenses of "gross indecency," which was punishable by two years imprisonment. This legislation was described as "the blackmailers' charter."

Contemporary English law in this field is essentially governed by the Sexual Offenses Act of 1956. Any sexual touching of a child of either sex under the age of sixteen is defined and punished as "indecent assault," regardless of whether the child resists or encourages the offense. The maximum penalty for buggery is life imprisonment, regardless of whether the victim solicited, consented to or resisted the behavior. Gross indecency is not defined but is an umbrella term to cover any kind of sexual activity between males of sixteen years or more.

Homosexual acts in public—for instance in parks—may also be prosecuted under local by-laws directed against indecent or offensive behavior. In London, the Hyde Park Regulations Act, 1932, provides that no person in the park shall "behave in any manner that is reasonably likely to offend against public decency. Penalty £5." Penalties under these laws are less, and the conviction is not so likely to attract publicity, since it does not distinguish between homosexual acts and such things as urinating outdoors or appearing inadequately clad. The Wolfenden Committee in Britain reported in favor of a relaxation of the laws against adult homosexuality, which ushered in the Sexual Offences Act, 1967. This act finally removed the penalties for homosexual acts in private between men over twenty-one. The act did not, however, deal with all Wolfenden's suggested reforms; all homosexual acts, whether buggery, gross indecency or attempts to procure gross indecency, committed by men over twenty-one with youths of sixteen up to twenty-one, even though the youth participates, are to incur penalties of up to five years imprisonment for the older man. For buggery or indecency with boys under sixteen, the existing penalties, including life imprisonment, remain unchanged. The act prescribes penalties for benefitting from the earnings of male prostitution and for procuring men for homosexual acts. Provisions against soliciting or importuning remain in force, and the acts will not be legally private if more than two persons are present. The Army, Air Force and Naval Discipline Acts remain in operation, excluding those individuals in the forces and at sea from the new freedom. Similarly, in most countries where consenting homosexuality is not criminal, if such conduct appears prejudicial to good military order it is dealt with as an internal disciplinary matter, for example, in the case of lesbianism in the women's services.

In the United States, recent advances in the decriminalization of homosexual behavior have occurred in the states of Colorado, Delaware, Oregon, Hawaii, Ohio, Illinois and Connecticut (Geis et al., 1976). Homosexual practices, provided they are private and between consenting adults, have been removed from the criminal code. The thrust for this leniency movement has arisen from demands by civil libertarian and gay activist groups. Homosexuals have been vocal in proclaiming their rights under equal protection legislation. Despite this, however, homosexuals in many parts of the United States are still subject to legal prosecution for indulging in their preferred sexual practice, and some practical difficulties experienced by homosexuals will be mentioned.

Self-proclaimed homosexuals may consistently be denied work because of discriminatory hiring policies, which have, of course, little relationship to the job requirement. Recently the Federal Civil Service has ruled that homosexual conduct cannot be used as the sole basis for disqualification from federal employment (Wetherbee and Coleman, 1976-1977). Despite this, however, a recent case ruled that a self-proclaimed gay clerk-typist could be dismissed from his position on the grounds that homosexuality was a "socially repugnant concept" and sufficient to terminate under Civil Service law. The armed forces maintain the additional threat of mandatory discharge for homosexuality.

Blackmail remains a distinct possibility despite recent legistion. Homosexuals indulging in clandestine activities continue to be afraid of reporting to authorities and accordingly succumb to blackmail as a ready means of escape. Sagarin and Mac-Namara (1975) suggest that those homosexuals who are inhibited from access to legal regress due to the precariousness of their position are victims of criminal violence more frequently than nonhomosexuals. The problem is exacerbated by the tendency of law enforcement agencies to focus undue attention on homosexuals and their activities to the extent that other more serious crimes may be left unattended (Geis et al., 1976).

Other problems arise in connection with child custody issues resulting from divorce actions where one parent is homosexual. In 1976 the California State Bar Association voted against a resolution recommending a parent's marital status or sexual orientation should not be considered an issue in child custody litigation (Coleman and Gaudard, 1977). Those who supported the California resolution argued that homosexuality was irrelevant to the issue of custody. Furthermore, it was felt that many Judges would misuse such information against the background of their own prejudices concerning sexual orientation.

Immigration regulations also continue to be a bone of contention for those homosexuals wishing to enter the United States. Section 212 (a) 4 of the United States Immigration and Nationality Act cites as ineligible to receive a visa "aliens inflicted with psychopathic personality or sexual deviation, or mental defect" (U.S. Immigration and Nationality Act of 1952, Rev. 1969). Accordingly, homosexuals may be excluded from admission to the United States solely on the grounds of sexual deviance. The only recourse such individuals have, should they persist in their desire to immigrate, would be to obtain a waiver of authority, which involves permission of the Attorney General with a recommendation by the Secretary of State. If this is granted, the alien may be admitted on a temporary basis as a nonimmigrant. The bureaucracy involved in such an action has led homosexuals to wonder if entry into "the land of the free" is worthy of their efforts. In an effort to declare such discrimination invalid, Clive Boutilier, a thirty-two-year-old Canadian-born individual who had worked for eight years in America, applied for United States citizenship and, in answer to the customary questions, reported that he had once been arrested for a homosexual act, although the charge had been dismissed. He was ordered to be deported on the grounds of "psychopathic personality." Supported by psychiatric evidence that he was not a psychopath, he took the case to the U.S. Court of Appeals, Second Circuit, in 1966, but it was rejected. In his ruling, Judge I. R. Kaufman described psychopathy as a vague rubric covering Congress's intent to bar all perverts. (*Time*, New York, 22 July 1966). The U.S. Supreme Court, on May 22, 1967, upheld the legality of deportation of alien homosexuals as psychopaths.

By way of contrast, the Canadian regulations appear to be less stringent. This is a reflection of the new Immigration Act passed in August of 1977 that no longer prohibits entry of an individual solely on the basis of his sexual orientation, as had been the case under previous immigration regulations.

Discriminatory sanctions against homosexuals have been a source of considerable public controversy in the United States. In the McCarthy witchhunting era, certain politicians attempted to obtain advantage by accusing their opponents of un-American activities, namely communist sympathies or homosexual tendencies—the two types of deviation being thought to go together. The Federal government accordingly became more cautious in the screening of their employees, and the risks involved in having homosexuals in the Foreign Service or engaged in secret work were widely publicized (GAP, 1955). Although the political and security risks arising from homosexuality have received less emphasis in recent times and in political debates, the argument nevertheless continues. In England, the Radcliffe Report on security in the public service suggests that every candidate for a post involving access to highly secret information should go through a positive vetting procedure that includes a check with the Security Service and "a field investigation into his character and circumstances." The report also mentioned that "irregular marital or sexual relations do not present themselves as necessarily the most dangerous traits from a security point of view." The report strongly advised transfer to a more innocuous post rather than discharge for staff who fail to obtain clearance (Radcliffe Report, 1962).

Another problem arises when an American serviceman admits to or is diagnosed as having homosexual tendencies, even though he may have committed no offense. In these cases he is promptly discharged "without honor" resulting in a forfeiture of his veteran's rights and financial benefits and subsequent possible difficulty in obtaining employment (Cory, 1960).

It is thus clear that if convicted, or once their condition becomes known to authority, homosexuals, like the lepers or the insane, must expect legal and social restrictions. If engaged in certain fields, such as teaching or government posts involving security risk, they will lose their jobs. If they belong to a profession with strict disciplinary codes, such as solicitors and physicians, they may have their license to practice removed. Such individuals will not be accepted for admission to the armed forces or the merchant navy and will be found unsuitable for a wide range of employment, such as police, prison service, youth workers and so forth. They will be denied access to important posts in political or public life. They may even encounter difficulties if they wish to enter as students to a university. They will be rejected if they apply to immigrate to another country. Such facts result in much resentment, for they underline the homosexual's inferior social status. Legislation also appears to operate unjustly, penalizing the comparatively well-behaved man whose condition happens to have come to official notice while leaving other more obvious homosexuals unmolested.

Transvestism

Transvestism by itself is not a criminal offense. It is the resultant effects of such behavior, however, that may on occasion conflict with the law. A high proportion of transvestites have a criminal record (James, 1969). The usual types of crime with which a transvestite is charged range from burglary, stealing and assault to being an idle and disorderly person found in female attire at a hotel for an unlawful person (English Vagrancy Act, 1824, Section 4) and loitering with intent. Transvestites may also be charged with offenses under the Servant's Characters Act, 1792. In this Act, an individual who dresses as a woman and then offers himself under false pretenses as a female servant may be charged and convicted. Many transvestites are apprehended when utilizing a public washroom or engaging in homosexual acts. Burglary and stealing, usually involving women's clothing and jewelry, by transvestites is often associated with fetishism.

In the United Kingdom, transvestites may be prosecuted for loitering with intent to commit an arrestable offense (Prevention of Crimes Act, 1871, S. 15 as amended by Criminal Law Act, 1967) or for being an idle or disorderly person being found on enclosed premises for an unlawful purpose that involves suspicious conduct (Vagrancy Act of 1824 S. 4).

Several interesting cases involving transvestites in England have been reported by James (1969). In *R. v. Barnard* (1837), a musician had dressed up as a woman in order to obtain employment in a lady's orchestra in a hotel. He was convicted on the grounds that he intended to defraud by dressing up and obtaining money by false pretenses.

Crossdressing has also been adopted to facilitate a sexual offense, such as a criminal assault on children. Such individuals, in addition to being prosecuted for indecent acts, etc., can also be charged with breaking the Child and Welfare Acts of their country.

Transvestites may appear in court on the grounds that they intended to defraud or blackmail others. Their disturbed behavior may also give rise to divorce proceedings, the grounds for a petition usually being cruelty. In the case of *Bohnel v. Bohnel* (1960, cited in James, 1969), the Court of Appeals affirmed the refusal of a decree of divorce for cruelty on the grounds of the husband dressing as a woman. In this case, the court held that the husband did not intend to injure his wife by crossdressing. Other cases might be decided differently today, particularly after the decision of the House of Lords in *Gollins v. Gollins* (1964), which removed the requirement of the intent element in cruelty cases.

Finally, transvestites who exhibit their garb and their genitals may be convicted for indecent exposure under a variety of statutes.

Transsexualism

A transsexual is confronted by a myriad of emotional, social and legal complications unparalleled in any other area of sexual deviance. The abovementioned legal issues concerning homosexuals and transvestites also apply to the transsexual. Such problems, however, represent the tip of an iceberg of difficulties encountered by those transsexuals seeking to undergo sex reassignment surgery. Some of the more important and fascinating medico-legal aspects will be discussed in the following section.

MEDICO-LEGAL ASPECTS OF SEX DETERMINATION

The law, which is essentially an artefact, is a system of regulations that depends upon precise definition. In contrast, medicine, which is a biological science, is dependent upon the facts of biology. Accordingly, the law is obliged to classify its material into exclusive categories, and being a binary system, its thrust is designed to produce conclusions of the "Yes" or "No" type. Unfortunately, biological phenomena cannot be reduced to exclusive categories, so that medicine is often unable to give "Yes" or "No" answers. It is this fundamental conflict that lies at the root of all medico-legal difficulties in this field (Ormrod, 1972).

The law is largely indifferent to sex and classifies an individual by his or her anatomic sex that is determined at birth. From a biological point of view, sex-change operations do not and cannot change the sex of an individual. Instead, they merely remove the physical attributes of one sex and construct imitations of the other. Transsexuals are genitally, gonadally and chromosomally male or female, as the case may be. It is only at the social level that there is a discrepancy between the sex whose role they have assumed and their physical structure. The law, therefore, views individuals whose physical appearance has been drastically altered by extensive surgery as psychologically abnormal males or psychologically abnormal females. When the decision is made to "assign" a patient to one sex or another, this creates legal difficulties from a practical perspective, for all the physician has done is to recommend a particular mode of living.

It could be argued that medical advances in the field of transsexuality have posed a difficult, if not insoluble, problem to the law, which must provide a "Yes" or "No," "man" or "woman" type of decision. In practice, however, the problem rarely arises. In the law of tort, sex is almost totally irrelevant, for it does not matter whether an injured plaintiff or a negligent defendant is a man or woman. The legal consequences are the same. The law of defamation, however, does differentiate between the sexes in that a woman whose chastity has been impugned is not required to prove that she has suffered actual loss, whereas a man must do so if he is to recover damages. In the law of contract, sex does not matter except possibly in life insurance, where the difference in the expectation of life between the sexes influences premiums. In the area of property law or settlement of a will, documentary identification is of crucial importance and will be considered in a later section. In the criminal law, sex is not important and is irrelevant to charges of dishonesty, stealing, fraud and similar offenses. It does not arise in cases of violence. There are some sexual offenses in which the sex of the victim or the accused is essential to the charge, e.g. rape or sexual intercourse without consent, or with a girl under the age of sixteen, or gross indecency between male persons. However, all cases of rape or of unlawful sexual intercourse are also indecent assault, which it is not necessary to establish the sex of either victim or assailant. It might be a defense to gross indecency (which does not involve an assault) to prove that one of the partners was a female.

Ormrod (1972), writing from a British perspective, regards family law as the only branch of the law in which problems of sex determination may arise, the validity of a marriage in particular being the important issue. To constitute a valid marriage, the parties must be of different sexes, for by definition a union between a man and a woman constitutes marriage. Inability to consummate the marriage means inability to have normal sexual intercourse and is a ground for annulment. Such an issue arose in the widely publicized case of *Corbett v. Corbett* (1970), better known as the April Ashley case. Ms. Ashley and Mr. Corbett had gone through a marriage ceremony in Gibraltar. Shortly after Mr. Corbett requested a declaration that there never had been a marriage at all on the grounds that April was a male. April was a male transsexual who had undergone surgical reconstruction before the ceremony. The legal issue was to determine April's true sex. It was contended that April was for all social purposes a woman in the sense that she had adopted a female role and had been "assigned" to the feminine gender and, accordingly, should be regarded as a woman for the purpose of marriage.

The Honourable Sir Roger Ormrod, who is a physician as well as a Judge of the Supreme Court of Judicature, concluded that in the context of marriage, April was a male. He reasoned that genitally, before the operation, the sex was male, i.e., there was evidence that there was a small but otherwise normal penis and no evidence of female genitalia either internal or external; gonadally before operation the sex was male, i.e. there was evidence that testes were present in the scrotum; chromosomally the sex was male because the Y chromosome was present in all the cells examined. Ormrod argued that the operation was irrelevant because the result was pure artefact.

In an address to the Medico-legal Society of the Royal Society of Medicine in 1972, Ormrod mentioned that if a decision ever had to be made in a matrimonial situation, he would regard the genital sex as decisive. This would provide the socially appropriate answer, although it would be quite wrong to regard the social criterion as in any way decisive in the matrimonial context. He felt that it would be easier to obtain a decree of nullity on the grounds of incapacity on the part of the woman than to embark on the exercise of sex determination. Ormrod felt that English courts will probably be able to evade the most awkward results of advancing medical knowledge and that the only people who would get tied in knots over difficult questions would be lawyers of the Ministry of Social Security who have to decide the difficult questions.

In spite of Ormrod's emphatic opinion that the law is indifferent to sex, it is clear that since 1952 when an American called George Jorgensen went to Denmark for surgery and became Christine Jorgensen, rigid sexual classifications have begun to blur. More recently, publicity has focused on a tennis star/physician, Doctor Renee Richards, who before sex reassignment was Doctor Richard Raskin. There is, unfortunately, no legal theory to turn to in determining how to fit this new third sexual category of the transsexual into the legal system. In a recent civil rights case, for example, a transsexual alleged that he was dismissed from his job as the result of sex discrimination after undergoing sex reversal (*Voyler v. Ralph K. Davies Medical Centre*, 1975)|. The court was at a loss in obtaining a solution for this plaintiff. A recent case in New Jersey, however, upheld a marriage between two biological males and required the husband to pay spousal support to the wife on the grounds that the male spouse had become physically, psychologically and anatomically female (*MT v. JT*, 1976). These recent decisions have occurred against a background where society refused to accept marriages between homosexuals on the grounds that lawful marriage requires members of the opposite sex. It underlines the grave judicial difficulties in coping with this man-made sexual category.

THE CRIME OF MAYHEM

Physicians have been afraid of patients who desired an anatomic cure for what appeared to be a psychological problem. Other physicians feared damage to their reputations, malpractice suits, suits for loss of consortium of the altered spouse or even criminal prosecution. In the minds of many physicians, the removal of healthy organs merely at the request of the patient may constitute battery or mayhem.

Criminal laws and medical licensing boards forbid treatment without sufficient medical indication and unwarranted removal of body parts. The crime of mayhem has an interesting history, an understanding of which is relevant to the issue of transsexual surgery.

In early common law, mayhem was committed only by inflicting an injury that reduced the victim's ability to fight. Willful maiming was a crime against the King as well as the victim, since the victim was rendered useless in combat. The crime deprived individuals of those parts that abated their courage. The loss of a tooth, ear or nose was not mayhem because they were not regarded as useful in a fight. The penalties for mayhem were derived from biblical justice: an eye for an eye. Individuals were sentenced to lose the like part, except for castration, which resulted in death or exile and the loss of one's estate to the King (Blackstone, 1803).

More recently, mayhem is generally regarded as a statutory offense that has shifted its emphasis from the military and combative effect of the injury to the preservation of the human body in normal functioning. The integrity of the person is now all-important (*U.S. v. Cook*, 1972). Mayhem statutes prohibit any act that "unlawfully and maliciously deprives a human being of a member of his body, or disables, disfigures, or renders it useless" (California Penal Code, Section 203). Castration is implicitly included, and no premeditation or specific intent to injure the particular member is required. General intent is presumed from the malicious and unlawful act.

Many statutes require "malice," a nebulous term referring to the defendant's state of mind. It is variously defined as "reckless or wanton disregard or indifference to the rights of others" (*U.S. v. Vollweiler*, 1964), the "act of a depraved and malicious spirit" (*Nestlerode v. U.S.*, 1941) or a state of mind "fatally bent on mischief and unmindful of social duties" (*Fryer v. U.S.*, 1953). Courts have, therefore, considered that the act of surgery itself may be criminal mayhem, despite the fact that effective surgical change from male to female requires castration (Belli, 1978).

Transsexual surgery is lawful in Belgium, Canada, Switzerland and Great Britain provided a thorough medical evaluation indicates that such surgery would be therapeutic and is conducted in good faith with reasonable skill. Holland and Denmark have established a medico-legal council that must first approve the requirements for surgery. The surgery remains unlawful in Germany and is a risky undertaking in Argentina. Indeed, in 1966 in Argentina, a surgeon was convicted of assault for performing a sex change; the patient's consent was considered invalid because of his emotional and mental immaturity and the fact that his neurotic craving for surgery made such consent involuntary. Other surgeons have been charged with aggravated assault for performing surgery on demand but have been acquitted on the technicality that patients involved were actually pseudohermaphrodites who received "sexual clarification" and not sex change (Smith, 1971).

In the United States the issue is far from resolved. In *Hartin v. Director of Bureau of Records* (1973), a New York court refused to order a new sex designation to appear on a transsexual's birth certificate and described sex reversal as "an experimental form of psychotherapy in which mutilating surgery is conducted on a person with the intent of setting his mind at ease." The court disapproved of "resolving a person's unhealthy mental state" by drastic surgery. In *Jessin v. the County of Shasta* (1969), a case that involved voluntary nontherapeutic sterilization, the court ruled that vasectomies do not constitute mayhem, for they do not render the patient impotent or unable to fight for the King; the court cited in support of the decision an earlier precedent set in the 1934 case of *Christensen v. Thornby*. This is somewhat surprising in the light of the fact that permanent impotency is the major goal of sex surgery.

Belli (1978) has raised some interesting medico-legal issues, believing that a physician would certainly be criminally liable for removing a healthy arm merely because a patient requested it. He suggests that therapeutic value may be the deciding factor. The problem arises, however, in the determination of therapeutic value. Like the patient with the perfectly acceptable nose who wants it made into a perfect nose, there may be no objective therapeutic value to a procedure, yet it may result in profound and lasting subjective changes in identity and improved self-esteem and daily functioning. Smith (1971) stresses that any drastic operation of a nontherapeutic nature is unlawful unless there is a justifiable reason for it, such as cosmetic surgery that will not endanger healthy organs or donation of an organ for transplant.

Because mayhem statutes vary from state to state, a physician should consult legal counsel before performing sexual assignmen surgery on males or females. North Carolina's mayhem statutes, for example, prohibit both malicious and nonmalicious "unlawful" maiming. The statutes may cover vasectomy and mastectomy as well as castration. It is wise to obtain a letter from the state Attorney General prior to surgery if the state's mayhem statute would appear to bar the operation. Even when the state's mayhem statute specifically prohibits castration and other disfigurement, the operation is legal when it is medically indicated, e.g. in hermaphroditism or in penile or breast cancer, and is properly performed. It is, therefore, possible that such procedures may be undertaken legally for transsexuals. Certainly the manifest benefit to the individual transsexual is a powerful argument that favors the legality of the sex reassignment operation when it is medically and psychiatrically indicated (Presser, 1977).

INFORMED CONSENT

Informed consent is becoming an increasingly important legal issue in sex reassignment surgery. The patient, selected in part on the basis of psychological health and therefore capable of consenting to such surgery, must, of course, be fully informed of the procedures to which he or she will be subjected and the probable and possible outcomes of the various surgical steps. Some interesting medico-legal dilemmas arise, however, when one considers the issue of informed consent. The question may be raised, how can a surgeon be charged with maliciously performing an act to which the patient consented? A possible analogy might be an abortion issue where jurisdictions are sharply divided. In some jurisdictions where abortion is regarded as criminal, the plaintiff may be considered an accomplice or participant in an unlawful act, and the court will therefore refuse to entertain an action arising from a criminal transaction. Other courts simply hold that consent to criminal abortion bars recovery for assault or battery (*Sayadoff v. Warda*, 1954). It is reasoned that antiabortion statutes are primarily for the protection of the unborn child and the public, not the woman, and thus there is no reason to compensate the woman for her voluntary act.

The abortion analogy, however, may be unsound, for the surgery does involve life other than the patient's. Sex-change operations affect no one but the patient, and it might be more reasonable to consider an elective sterilization as the model for the courts to adopt.

Physicians may assume that because they obtained an informed consent they will be protected from criminal prosecution for mayhem. Physicians should, however, bear in mind that their act may also amount to a breach of the public peace as well as an injury to a private person. The case of *State v. Fransua* (1973) established that one cannot apply consent to an act that disturbs the peace and dignity of the state to justify a criminal act. Similarly, one cannot consent to a shooting, a beating (*State v. Roby*, 1909) or being sadistically burned by someone with a cigarette (*Commonwealth v. Farrell*, 1948). Courts have also held that one cannot consent to any assault or battery that is likely to cause great bodily harm. In the case of *Commonwealth v. Farrell* (1948), consent was found to be immaterial when there is "any hurt or injury calculated to interfere with the health or comfort of the victim."

It could be argued that such court decisions are inappropriate to transsexuals. Transsexual surgery is private and discreet and affects no one but the patient. It does not involve the public peace, and there is no bodily harm that interferes with the victim's health. Indeed, the majority of transsexuals report great improvement in all aspects of their lives after surgery. From a legal point of view, therefore, there is little reason to prosecute the surgeon for a requested surgery done in good faith. All this assumes that surgery is conducted with reasonable skill, in good faith, and with informed consent. It goes without saying, of course, that surgery in the absence of a valid informed consent or beyond the scope of consent is technical assault and battery or mayhem (*Berkey v. Anderson*, 1970). Malpractice suits will always be available for negligently performed procedures.

Resolution of many of the above issues is, of course, still to be decided in the courts. The potential legal hazard confronting a surgeon who is deciding whether to operate is the question of the validity of a transsexual's consent for surgical sex reversal. Consent requires an affirmative act of an unconstrained and undeceived will (*People ex rel Burke v. Steinberg*, 1947). Elsewhere in this volume a transsexual's desire to have surgery has been described as a craving, an obsession and a passion. The question that arises, therefore, is how can consent to surgery be valid when such a desire is a symptom of psychological illness? Such a question has also yet to be decided by the courts. In this connection the case of *People v. Samuels* (1967) is of interest.

Here the defendant was charged with assault and battery, which was apparent from viewing the film. The court, however, argued that this was only an apparent consent that lacked real legal validity. The judge considered the masochistic victim to be suffering from a mental disorder that compelled him to submit to beatings: "a normal person in full possession of his faculties is not free to consent to the use, upon himself, of force likely to produce great bodily injury" (quoted in Belli, 1978). Such a decision is surprising in light of the fact that candidates are selected for surgery on the basis of lack of substantial psychopathology. The legal dilemma, therefore, arises that if a person passionately desires surgery, he or she is considered mentally ill and cannot have it, but if an individual does not crave surgery quite as intensely, he or she is mentally competent and can, therefore, undergo it.

The Gender Identity Committee at John Hopkins Hospital has suggested the following criteria in the selection of patients for possible sex reassignment surgery (Money and Schwartz, 1965).

1. The patient must have lived in the desired sex vocationally and socially for a long enough period of time to prove his (or her) ability to function in society in the changed sex.
2. The patient must be at least twenty-one years of age.
3. The patient must have a clean police record, though impersonation convictions are allowable.
4. If the patient had a history of temporal lobe epilepsy, he would require a neurosurgical workup, with a view to relief of both seizure and psychosexual symptoms.
5. The patient must be legally free of any previous marriage bond.
6. The patient must live within accessible travelling distance to the hospital in order to ensure conscientious follow-up.
7. The patient must designate a next of kin as an additional informant willing to give written operative consent. The reason for this rule is to safeguard against erroneous personal and social history giving, to safeguard against malpractice charges on the part of the next of kin, to have

the guarantee of at least minimal family acceptance of the operated patient should there arise an emergency in the future and to improve the social chances of rehabilitation.

Essentially, the physician makes his selection primarily on the basis of behavioral and psychological data, relying extensively on clinical judgment.

THE RIGHT TO PRIVACY AND SURGERY

The right to privacy and the right to treatment have recently become important legal issues. The case of *Griswold v. Connecticut* (1965) declared the laws forbidding use of contraceptives unconstitutional. This has created a climate of opinion that involves the sanctity and privacy of the marital relationship. *Roe v. Wade* (1973) also recognized a right of personal privacy in decisions about marriage, procreation, contraception and even abortion. *Jessin v. County of Shasta* (1969) included voluntary nontherapeutic sterilization within the zone of privacy, and *In re Lifschutz* (1970) went further and extended intimacy in interpersonal relations in individual marriages to professional and group situations.

The climate has, therefore, been established that one has a right to make decisions about procreation and contraception, and it would follow logically that individuals have the right to choose their ultimate birth control. To date, however, individuals who have been rejected for surgery and have demanded the right to surgery have had no success in convincing hospitals or courts that sex reversal is their legal right (Mehl, 1973).

The right to surgery does not yet exist, and sex-change operations are not available on demand from reputable clinics. The grim saga that existed when abortion was unlawful should emphasize the fact that penalties never deterred those who really desired an abortion. Individuals in such situations turned to dangerous and unsanitary methods in hidden backroom abortion factories, in contrast to the rich, who went abroad and payed large sums of money for the privilege. A similar situation may be occurring with those individuals who desire sex change.

Belli (1978) reports his experience with individuals who have received sex changes in "bargain basements." The damage inflicted by inferior procedures and inadequate selection and counselling he regards as horrifying. Laub and Fisk (1974) have also described frustrated individuals who, when denied surgery, have taken matters into their own hands and turned to self-mutilation and suicide. As with abortion or cosmetic surgery, a qualified right to do what we wish with our own bodies should be recognized. The state, of course, has to intervene with some regulations to ensure that surgery is carried out with skill and in good faith.

In Canada, there have been no test cases, but Hoenig (1974) suggests that gender reassignment surgery would be legal under Section 45 of the Canadian Criminal Code, provided that the patient is in distress and would benefit from the treatment. Discussion has recently arisen around the question of whether such reassignment operations should be covered by the provincial insurance schemes in certain Canadian provinces. In Britain, the operation is covered by the National Health Insurance scheme.

POSTOPERATIVE LEGAL ASPECTS

The completion of surgical reassignment marks the beginning, not the end, of the transsexual's encounters with the legal system (Smith, 1971). The changing of documentary identification becomes an emotional necessity, for the transsexual's name is inappropriate and must be changed; his birth certificate states the wrong sex; his passport has the wrong picture and name in it; his Social Security card must be altered so that he may secure employment in the new sex. The establishing of an automobile license, charge accounts, credit cards, a license to practice law, medicine and so forth are fraught with difficulties. It is, therefore, necessary for the transsexual to create a new and present identity with as little reference to the past as possible. The transsexual's initial and main concern centers around this need for new identification, and practical difficulties experienced by transsexuals in altering documentary identification will be discussed in the following sections.

Change of Name

The transsexual has often undergone a name change prior to surgery (Hoenig et al., 1970). The procedures by which this can be done vary from country to country and are relatively easy. One may change his or her name at will, provided there is no fraudulent intent or prejudice to others. In Canada, the United States or the United Kingdom, it is not necessary to apply for a "legal" change of name and it is acceptable simply to assume a new name. However, it is of practical significance to obtain a court-decreed name change because of the facilitating effect that this has upon subsequent procedures involved in birth certificate or other documentary amendments.

Most transsexuals have, in fact, already been living under and using a name that more closely relates to their assumed new sexual identity.

The timing of the lawyer's application for a name change is important, for if the individual is not crossdressing in his chosen gender, has not received hormone therapy and has not undergone surgical sex reassignment, the court may well turn down the application on the basis that the applicant has not advanced a sufficient reason for the change of name (Nelson et al., 1976). In the absence of these conditions the court is likely to err on the side of caution, out of a fear of fraud or misrepresentation, and reject the application (Moore et al., 1970).

In some jurisdictions, application for a name change must be published in a newspaper before the matter can proceed, e.g. The Ontario Change of Name Act, 1970. There is also a provision in the Act that allows the court to dispense with such a requirement if affidavit evidence is presented that sets out sufficient reasons requesting dispensation of publication. Similarly, private hearings may be arranged in the judge's chambers as a method of proceeding with as little publicity as possible.

As a general rule, the individual's application should be supported by any available medical evidence, in affidavit form, from his psychiatrist, surgeon and endocrinologist. Such affidavits should establish the individual's chosen gender identity, the name by which he is commonly known, the operations that have been performed and the results of hormone therapy as well as the general prognosis.

Birth Certificates

Altering the transsexual's birth certificate is very important, for it is a basic document of gender identification that may have to be produced when seeking employment, purchasing insurance, obtaining travel documents, as proof of age and so forth. The alteration of a birth certificate, and in particular the change in designated sex, is usually difficult, if not impossible, to obtain (Nelson et al., 1975; Sherwin, 1969). In litigated cases the courts have held, in effect, that a birth certificate is just what it is, a birth certificate. That is to say, it is a certification of a set of facts that were held true at the time of the person's birth, inclusive of the sex at the time of birth. In certain jurisdictions, amendments have been allowed, establishing that at the present time, or from a certain date, an individual is of an altered sex and known by an altered name. However, since the original birth certificate cannot be destroyed or obliterated, such amendments do not serve the purpose of creating a new identity. Indeed, an amended birth certificate acts as a constant reminder of the past (Hoenig, 1977).

In most countries, a change in the birth certification can be made only if it is established that a mistake had been made at the time of the original issue of the certificate, e.g. Ontario's Vital Statistics Act, Section 30(2), 1970. Similar legislation exists in the United States and Britain. Nowhere is it clearly established how the sex of the newborn is to be determined; the decision is usually left to the doctor or the midwife (Holloway, 1974).

Two Canadian provinces, British Columbia and Alberta, have recently passed legislation that allows a registration of change of sex following sex reassignment surgery (Nelson et al., 1976). Two interesting decisions have also recently been reported in the United States (Smith, 1971; Walton, 1974). In *Anonymous v. Weiner* (1966), a male-to-female transsexual after surgery applied to the New York City Department of Health's Bureau of Records and Statistics for a suitable change of "her" birth certificate. The Department turned for advice to the New York Academy of Medicine, which in turn sought the opinion of a panel of medical and legal experts. The panel opposed the change on the grounds that male-to-female transsexuals were still chromosomally males. The panel also questioned whether laws and records such as the birth certificate should be changed and thereby used as a means to help "psychologically ill" persons in their social adaptation.

Holloway (1968) has criticized this ruling on the grounds that sex is not always determined by chromosomes. He was distressed by the court's decision not to assist the transsexual in this way and pointed out that no conceivable harm could possibly come to anyone as a result of such a change.

The case of *In re Anonymous* (1968) adopted a much more humane approach and strongly criticized the decision reached in *Anonymous v. Weiner*. The court discounted the notion that fraud would be perpetrated upon the public if the change was allowed and stated, "Should the question of a person's identity be limited by the results of mere histological section or by chemical analysis, with a complete disregard for the human brain, the organ responsible for most functions and reactions, many so exquisite in nature, including sex orientation? I think not."

In the United States, fifteen states have permitted post-operative changes in the birth records (Smith, 1971). In the remaining states, the transsexual has to go through life with a female gender identity, "female" external genitalia, and an embarrassing basic personal document, describing "her" as a male. In the United Kingdom, as mentioned above, a number of patients have obtained a changed birth certificate and, although less than satisfactory for the transsexual, it does help to a certain extent. In Germany, the personal status remains unchanged by the operation (Uhlenbruck, 1969). Legislation has been more enlightened in Switzerland, for as early as 1945 in the case of *In re Leber*, the Swiss Board concluded that gender identity was the proper criterion for determining sex in an operated transsexual.

It is clear, therefore, that a changed birth certificate is of

great importance to the reassigned transsexual, and for all
practical purposes, it serves as a legal determination of sex.
Future enlightened court decisions are awaited with interest.

Other Documents

Following name and birth certificate changes, the transsexual
is confronted by need to alter a host of other documents—
driver's license, credit cards, passport, social insurance card,
bank accounts, school records, university degrees and diplomas,
professional licenses and citizenship papers, etc. A legal, rather
than a common law, name change will enhance the transsexual's
ability to successfully negotiate with the officials required in
these transactions. Statutory declarations, setting out the situation for name change, will facilitate the obtaining of the desired
changes.

A number of time-consuming and complicated maneuvers
may, however, be required in negotiating documentary changes.
For example, a male-to-female transsexual, who in his former
male role obtained a Ph.D. degree in the field of biochemistry
and had been previously engaged in several responsible employment positions prior to sex reassignment surgery, now, as a
female, may wish to seek employment in her specialty field.
In attempting to establish that she is a qualified biochemist,
she will have to present academic records, awards, degrees and
letters of reference supporting her credentials for employment.
In such cases, universities may be reluctant to alter or make
changes in scholastic records and degrees despite affidavits from
the individual's lawyer and physician. Universities, although
sympathetic to the predicament of such individuals, may themselves be caught in the dilemma of whether or not they should
inform the prospective employer of the former identity of the
applicant (Sherwin, 1969). It is likely that if the university
feels obliged to inform the prospective employer of the transsexual's background, employment would be denied. In such
instances the transsexual's attorney should clarify with the university that they are only being requested to provide a record
of the academic accomplishments of the individual and have

not been requested to make a personal recommendation or vouch for the individual's mental or physical health; indeed, such concern is beyond their scope.

Other situations may be described as farcical. In some provinces in Canada, the Department of Welfare, before issuing a female social insurance card, requires a transsexual applicant to sign a document waiving rights to maternity benefits (Hoenig, 1974). In the United States, the Social Security Administration has advised that "a legal opinion will be required in the case of an individual applying for widow's or other benefits if his sex is other than that on the original social security card, even though the name on the records has been changed" (Presser, 1977). It should also be mentioned that the transsexual's partner is eligible to be paid spouse's or survivor's benefits if his or her postoperative marriage is valid under the laws of the state in which the insured was living at the time of application or when the insured died, or if the spouse would be entitled to participate in the distribution of the insured intestate property under state law.

Sex-reassigned individuals are exempt from the armed services. Formerly male transsexuals cannot serve in the military's male branches and are medically disqualified from the Women's Army Corps. A similar situation applies to formerly female transsexuals. Despite this, the Civil Rights Act of 1964 protects against sex discrimination in employment. Such legislation should help provide job opportunities and security to transsexuals. In addition federal grants are available to state vocational rehabilitation agencies to provide vocation-related rehabilitative services to persons "with a physical or mental disability who need help in obtaining and holding an appropriate job." Several states have also provided assistance to transsexuals, including help in obtaining employment, and have categorized their problem as a "psychiatric disability" (Presser, 1977).

Creating an identity is very difficult and therefore requires careful planning by the transsexual and his lawyer. There is no standard procedure involved in altering documents. Each case is unique and requires inventive methods of response.

Marital and Family Considerations

A marriage between a preoperative transsexual and a member of the opposite anatomical sex is valid. In several states, however, such marriages must be dissolved before reassignment surgery is undertaken. If one partner subsequently becomes the same sex as the other, the marriage may either remain valid, or become void by operation of law, or be voidable, or provide grounds for divorce; the possibilities vary from state to state. If the marriage becomes void, any children would be of the "valid period" of the marriage, and the date of voiding the marriage would probably be determined by the date of surgical reassignment.

Most states do not require any proof of sex before granting a marriage license. Problems may arise, however, if the spouse later wishes to terminate the relationship. Before a postoperative transsexual marries a person of the newly opposite sex, he or she should disclose the surgical reassignment and the resulting sterility to avoid any subsequent charge of fraud or grounds for annulment or divorce (Presser, 1977). Similarly, impotence may be a ground for annulment or divorce in many jurisdictions. If the inability to perform coitus as a male was revealed prior to marriage, impotence would not be a ground for annulment but a ground for divorce only.

The medico-legal aspects surrounding sex determination as they involve marriage have been mentioned previously in the British case of *Corbett v. Corbett.* The validity of transsexual marriages, and especially those occurring after sex reassignment surgery, has not yet been litigated in Canada. In the United States, however, in March, 1976, the New Jersey Appellate Division of the Superior Court unanimously declared that the individual who changes sex through surgery is entitled to all the legal rights enjoyed by others of the same sex, including marriage. The court also ruled that the marriage of a transsexual would be valid as long as the transsexual had told the partner in advance about the sex-change operation. Interestingly, the court rejected previous court rulings in the United States and England, including that in *Corbett v. Corbett* (Erickson, 1976). The New Jersey Supreme Court denied a request for further appeal, and so the judgment, at the time of this writing, still stands. The legal situation once again underlines the profound uncertainties that beset the lives of transsexuals, whose precarious position may repeatedly be tested and retested in the courts.

When a transsexual marries someone who already has custody of the children of a previous marriage, it is unlikely that any problems will arise that would affect the custody or adoption situation. However, if the couple should seek to adopt children after their marriage, the question of fitness may be brought forward by an adoption agency or if the court learns of the history of the transsexual partner. The recent case of *Randall* (*formerly Christian*) *v. Christian* dealt with this issue. The state court allowed a sexually reassigned transsexual to retain custody of children born prior to the operation. Gay Christian had obtained a divorce from her husband, Doctor Duane Christian, in 1964 and was awarded custody of her four daughters. She subsequently underwent sex reassignment, took the name of Mark Randall and married a woman. The judge concluded that in this custody case the children understood the sex change and that their welfare would "be best served by placing them with their former mother, and now the father-image, Mark Randall."

It appears that the climate of public policy is tending to favor recognizing the marriage of postoperative transsexuals, since the right to marry is considered a vital right in the United States. The future may permit an individual who looks, acts and perceives himself or herself to be of one sex to marry a person of the opposite sex.

Criminal Aspects

A transsexual's activity often resembles certain forms of behavior that are defined as crimes in the criminal statutes. In many jurisdictions in the United States, impersonating a female or masquerading as such renders a male liable to criminal prosecution under vagrancy or disorderly conduct laws. There is, of course, a striking difference between these activities. The transsexual dresses as a female because he feels that he is a female, and in no sense of the word, therefore, is he impersonating or masquerading (Sherwin, 1969). Despite this, however, transsexuals have been convicted.

A person's right to crossdress is not subject to criminal prosecution except when he attempts to commit an indictable offense, at which stage he may be prosecuted under the Canadian Criminal Code of forming the intent to commit an indictable offense while being disguised. Nelson et al. (1976) have suggested that, in order to forestall difficulties with the police, a transsexual should carry a letter from a physician that sets out an explanation of the transsexual's condition.

The transsexual may also be subject to the same legal difficulties that confront homosexuals, as mentioned previously. The transsexual may be charged, under certain circumstances, for buggery or gross indecency, acts that to her are but normal sexual activities not normally chargeable when carried out by a man and a woman. The anomalous situation has been succinctly summaried by Walton (1974): "male adulterers should be heartened by the fact that they may indulge in cunnilingus, copula crura, per oram, per anum and even per vaginam—perennially ad nauseam and with impunity. It is open season on transsexuals."

Other legal anomalies currently exist. For example, can a man be charged with raping a male-to-female transsexual? Similarly, can a male who undergoes sex reassignment surgery be subject to indecent assault? These and other questions await adjudication.

In summary, the transsexual, having no appropriate law to live by, must learn to live without the law and, above all, to avoid becoming entangled with an inappropriate law (Sherwin, 1969).

Wills and Inheritances

Common laws relating to wills and inheritances may also pose difficulties for the transsexual. A will written prior to a transsexual's surgical sex reassignment that has designated him or her by the former name and relationship will usually allow the transsexual to claim the intended inheritance. If the bequest is made to a limited class, e.g. "my sons" or "my nieces," it is divided among the members of the class in existence at the time of the testator's death. Similarly, a bequest to "my younger son" or "my oldest daughter," with no name given, might not go to the intended legatee. It is, therefore, prudent that a person wishing to leave a bequest to a transsexual execute or reexecute the will to read "my daughter (or friend), Jane Smith, formerly John Smith." It would appear that the fundamental rule in considering the language of the will is to place on the words used the meaning that, having regard to the terms of the will, the testator intended. The question is not what the testator meant to do when s/he made the will but what the written words s/he used mean in the particular case (Nelson et al., 1976).

The problems of inheritance are further compounded by the fact that transsexuals are often excluded by their families following surgery or are regarded with shame and disgust. In such cases, although the deceased parent intended the transsexual to be the beneficiary, a relative may legally oppose the transsexual's inheritance.

The family may also question testamentary capacity of a transsexual on the grounds that s/he lacked the requisite mental capacity to execute a valid will. Such cases, however, await testing in court.

CONCLUSION

The foregoing review has shown that the legal status of the transsexual can at all times and in all respects be questioned in court. The transsexual is required to fight many battles in order to regularize his social and legal status. The situation is confusing and thoroughly unsatisfactory. Leo Abse, addressing the British House of Commons, has sympathetically and succinctly described the legal limbo that transsexuals are left to live in:

> We would be unjust and unfair if we persisted in continuing to believe that nature is not often shamelessly untidy. We have in our community a small group of people on whom nature has played a tragic trick. We would indeed be an insensitive parliament if we allowed the passing of this bill without amendment for that would push these people yet further into a bewildering limbo (Hansard, 814:118:1827 ff.).

Because our laws have been framed and applied with the traditional concepts of male and female in mind, transsexuals will continue to experience difficulties unless legislative recognition of sex reassignment after surgery is established. It is hoped that the legal and medical communities and society in general will become increasingly aware of the importance of gender reassignment to the productive life of the transsexual and that such individuals will also be entitled to the benefits each member of society expects and receives under the law.

CHAPTER 7

THE SURGICAL TREATMENT OF TRANSSEXUALITY

Norman B. Barwin

"She shall be called woman because she was taken out of man."
Genesis 2:23

INTRODUCTION

THE MALE TRANSSEXUAL represents but one variety of gender dysphoria, presenting himself to the gender team with apparently normal male physical genitalia and development. He feels he is a "woman in a man's body." He has an unwavering desire for castration, penectomy and construction of a vagina and labia. The selection of the proper patient while still intact for these operations and the evolution of the ideal surgical technique is still incomplete. The role of surgery in the treatment of these patients is as yet unproven, but much has already been learned about human behavior from surgery on the transsexual patient and much more will be learned in the future.

In discussing possible sex conversion surgery, a number of limitations must be emphasized (Baker, 1969). Modern surgery is not yet able to accomplish certain goals. The surgically treated patient will not be able to obtain a uterus or ovaries, nor will she be able to become pregnant. Permanent and prolonged use of estrogens is necessary to maintain female hormone levels. Many members of society will not relate to the transsexual as a normal female, even after successful conversion surgery (Barwin, 1976). Training in voice, deportment and dress may be required. It is most important that the patient be aware that surgical complications do result in some instances following the operation; these may entail additional surgery and may even reduce the quality of the final result. Both patient and surgeon must

127

be realistic about the achievements of modern reconstructive surgery.

A modern multidisciplinary gender identity team will aid the psychological, social and physical success in the properly selected and cooperative transsexual patient (Edgerton and Meyer, 1973). The procedure would include removal of the male genitalia and construction of an adequate vagina that will permit normal intercourse with a male and in many instances permit the patient to experience orgasm. Female breast contour can be successfully produced by hormone therapy and surgical mammoplasty. Unwanted facial hair can usually be controlled. The appropriate use of feminizing hormones will produce beneficial effects both psychologically and physically (Money and Wolfe, 1973).

It is definitely easier at the present time to produce feminization of the male transsexual than masculinization of the female transsexual (Money and Wolfe, 1973).

CRITERIA FOR SELECTION OF PATIENT SUITABLE FOR SURGERY

Accuracy of Diagnosis

Detailed psychiatric and psychological evaluation of the patient with gender dysphoria is essential. A gender team of psychiatrists, social workers, an endocrinologist, a surgeon and even the patient as an active member must accept the responsibility of long-term follow-up of any patient accepted for reconstructive surgery. There should be no attempt at solo selection, and the gender team, particularly the psychiatrist, should provide objectivity, backing and postoperative support for the patient.

Motivation of the Patient

The male transsexual patient often presents himself with disgust for any features of "maleness" and generally reads much on the subject of transsexualism (Edgerton and Meyer, 1973). Most are so well motivated that they are willing to undergo any amount of surgery, although they reluctantly accept a long continued program of psychotherapy. Transsexuals are often offended by any homosexual attractions to them. Most transsexuals tend to be "more feminine" than normal females on psychological testing and desperately wish to be viewed as normal heterosexual females (Green, 1970).

Age

Green (1970) states that it is too early to determine what will be the ultimate adult diagnosis of "feminine boys." At the University of Ottawa, the age distribution for patients seeking transsexual surgery has been between twenty-one and fifty-six years of age. The majority (approximately 70%) of patients presenting for surgery are between twenty-two and thirty-five years of age.

Family Support

The importance of encouragement, support and companionship during the postoperative period cannot be emphasized enough, as it is crucial that a close friend or member of the family, with the patient's knowledge, agree to provide assistance during the important adjustment period. Patients feel very much alone during this type of surgery. At the gender clinic, the author and his colleagues tend to reject married couples or parents with young children, but with further study this may prove invalid.

Potential for Follow-up

Although no guarantees can be given for follow-up, it is at least important for the corrected male transsexual to be willing to present herself for periodic postoperative evaluation of the breasts after implant surgery, of the vagina and retained male prostate, and of urinary function (Edgerton and Meyer, 1973). Psychiatric follow-up concerning post-operative adjustments, attitudes and emotions of the patient may yield data for interpretation and use of future patients. It is understandable that the surgically corrected male transsexual would like to eliminate all the unhappy past associations of the former male role; nevertheless, a certain amount of follow-up is essential.

TIMING OF SURGERY

Inevitably when the untreated male transsexual presents to a gender clinic seeking surgery, the timing of surgery is immediately raised. Provided the diagnosis has been properly established and there is good family support, suitable intelligence and economic status and a trial period of crossdressing and working in the feminine role, surgery can be planned. It is imperative that full psychiatric assessment, analysis and therapy be established before contemplating surgery. Furthermore, a test period on hormone therapy must be given for at least six months to a year (Baker, 1969). Various regimens have been recommended:

Diethylstilbesterol (Edgerton, 1974)	: 0:25-0:50 mg daily
Premarine	: 1.25 mg 4-5 times daily
DES + Medroxy progesterone (Edgerton, 1974)	: 0.25-2.5 mg daily
Estynil (Baker, 1969)	: 0.5 mg daily

The male transsexual feels "more relaxed" on estrogen therapy in addition to the benefits of estrogen on breast development and skin quality (Edgerton, 1974). During this trial period impotency results, which further aids in the acceptance of the female role. Furthermore, there is a general reduction of both penile and testicular size.

The most reliable and important indication for surgery is successful living in the female role without the benefits of surgical conversion (Randall, 1969).

Continued assessment by the gender teams is imperative, and preoperative support and interrogation is critical before such a major irreversible procedure is undertaken (Randall, 1969). It has been the policy of the clinic to show the patient diagrams of the procedure so that anxieties and fears can be reduced.

The patient must gain the emotional support necessary to aid in strengthening her feminine image from the surgeon and psychiatrist as well as from nonmedical people in her daily relationships (Randall, 1969).

SURGICAL TECHNIQUES FOR CONSTRUCTION
OF FEMALE GENITALIA

In the 1950s, simple castration and amputation of the male genitalia produced apparent subjective relief and satisfaction (Baker, 1969; Lipshultz and Corriere, 1976). With improved techniques and knowledge of vaginal reconstruction, transsexual patients have uniformly requested this as a primary or secondary procedure. It is important to stress that, although the transsexual will have the ability to engage in coitus satisfactorily following vaginal construction, orgasm may not always be possible.

The male transsexual may present for surgery having had no prior surgery or having had unsuccessful surgery or attempted self-amputation or castration. The latter presentation may create a difficult surgical problem with poorer functioning results. Ideally, the vagina should be lined with moist elastic and hairless skin. The diameter of the new vagina should be 4 cm, with a 10-14 cm depth. The lateral walls and perineum should contain sufficient sensation to provide satisfactory erotic stimulus during coitus.

The author has had most successful results in transsexual vaginal reconstruction using the modified penile flap technique of Edgerton and Bull (1974). The major advantage of this method is the utilization of the skin and subcutaneous tissue of the male penis by inverting it into a perineal jacket while maintaining the blood supply from the scrotal pedicle. A mobile vagina 16 cm in depth is achieved, and often a postoperative mold is not required. The scrotal tissue is thus preserved and used for the production of the labia and clitoris (see Figs. 8-1 through 8-10). Edgerton (1974) delays this stage of the procedure for three to four weeks, but the author has found that, provided the lateral pudendal arteries are preserved and the long pedicle flap delicately handled, fairly successful labia can be reconstructed at the time of initial surgery (Edgerton and Bull, 1970). However, if done as a one-stage technique, a vaginal form should be used to prevent contraction of circumference of the new vagina.

Following previous unsuccessful surgery or self-castration, the penile or scrotal tissue is no longer available. Using the modified McIndoe (1950) technique, a split-thickness graft is used from the thigh and the perineal jacket created. A cylindrical mold containing a split-thickness graft or its outer surface is inserted into the perineal jacket. The disadvantage is that of postoperative scarring and that a vaginal mold is required to be worn constantly for approximately six months. The technique also fails to provide for construction of the labia or clitoris.

The Jones-Hoopes-Schirmer technique (1968) involves the use of the hair-bearing scrotal skin for the walls of the new vagina. Unfortunately, there is often insufficient scrotal skin to provide adequate depth to the new vagina.

Some surgeons have recommended the use of a segment of colon isolated from the intestine for the new vagina (Edgerton, 1974). The major drawback of this technique is the continued chronic secretion of mucus from the new vagina. In the tunnelling of the cavity for the construction of the new vagina, it is important that dissection up to the level of reflexion of the pelvic peritoneum be carried out. The assistance of a urologist is most helpful for this stage of the procedure, as the dissection must be made above the rectourethrals to avoid injury to the anterior wall of the rectum (Barwin, 1976). The author utilizes a gloved finger within the rectum to prevent rectal injury. Preservation of the pudendal arteries, laterally and posteriorly, is crucial if the pedicle flap technique is to be used. A Foley catheter in the urethral disc reduces damage to the urethra and reduces the complication of urethrovaginal fistula. A superfistric aptostomy may be used postoperatively to prevent the Foley catheter from pressing against the underlying surface of the pubis and the resulting fistula formation (Edgerton, 1974).

Postoperative molds, stents or dressings should be applied in an exacting fashion to the newly created vagina. Avoidance of compression and great pressure is recommended. Heyer-Schulte Corporation has introduced a compressible vaginal stent made of foam rubber with a valve to prevent undue pressure.

More recently, McRoberts (Edgerton, 1974) described the

use of the scrotal flap to construct the posterior vaginal wall and a free skin graft to form the anterior wall. He furthermore suggests that transferring the coppora cavernosa of the penis to positions on either side of the new vagina will result in additional turgescence and stimulation within the newly created vagina.

Lipshultz and Carriere (1976) described a one-stage technique involving penectomy, orchidectomy and shortening of the male pendulous urethra to the midbulbous region. Reconstruction of the neovagina involved invagination of the penile skin to create the vaginal vault and utilization of the glans penis to form a cervix at the vault. The remaining urethra is used to establish a supravaginal meatus, while an erectile pseudoclitoral organ is established from the strips of the corpora cavernosa and labia are created from the relocated scrotal skin. To maintain adequate depth, a vaginal stent must be continuously worn for at least four to six weeks postoperatively and intermittently thereafter unless periodic sexual intercourse has begun.

With further improvements and refinements of the surgical processes involved in rehabilitating the male transsexual, consistent adequate anatomic results will be obtained with an acceptable rate of complications. Principal problems seen include rectovaginal fistula, urethrovaginal fistula, tenderness of the urethra, failure of skin graft to "take," hair growth in the vagina, vaginal stenosis, contraction of vaginal entrance, and a vagina too short or too small. This is often the consequence of failure to properly use a postoperative form or stent for a sufficient period of time.

OTHER SURGICAL PROCEDURES IN THE MALE TRANSSEXUAL

Breast Augmentation—Hormonal and Surgical

Although removal of the male genitalia and vaginal construction is of paramount importance to the male transsexual, it is sometimes wise to defer this irreversible procedure until the gender identity team has eliminated any uncertainty about surgical change. It may be prudent to complete more reversible partners of the surgical program first and to rate the effect of the dangers or the patient's adjustments and motivations for further surgery. Breast augmentation greatly increases the subjective feelings of femininity and should sometimes precede the genitovaginal surgery. The use of estrogens with transsexuals will not infrequently cause significant enlargement of breast size. In many cases, patients have reported breast enlargement with hormone therapy was sufficient for them to feel no further need for surgical treatment for breast enlargement. When surgery is required, preformed surgical breast implants have been found to be the most satisfactory. The results of these implants have proven to be highly successful from the standpoint of both appearance and general health of the patient.

Reduction Rhinoplasty

This procedure must be designed so that the ultimate size and contour of the nose will match naturally the remaining features of the patient's face. This procedure can be utilized as one of the feminizing operations on the male transsexual, but care must be taken not to alter nasal contours or size too greatly, as patients may experience a sense of "loss of identity" with associated postoperative crisis (Money and Wolfe, 1973).

Feminization of the Larynx

Male transsexuals may be embarrassed by large, rather exposed "Adam's apples." Reduction of laryngial cartilages may be possible, but it is not without hazard, as hoarseness or weakness of the voice may result. Most transsexuals will be able to develop a suitable soft and feminine voice by self-teaching techniques. Estrogens may also alter voice tone, although the mechanism of action is unclear.

Orthopedic Procedures in the Male Transsexual

Height or ankle thickness is of concern to some transsexuals, as they feel that this reflects a masculine appearance. Shortening of limbs in the excessively tall patient can be utilized but often requires many months of casting or immobilization and should only be considered after careful discussion with the patient as to the expected objectives.

Removal of Hair from Face and Body

Most male transsexuals are troubled by the presence of male hair pattern on the face, forearm or chest. Electrolysis carried out by a skilled technician will often offer the most suitable solution (Randall, 1969). X-ray therapy or "wax" treatments should be avoided. Estrogens appear to be valuable and further the long-term control of undesirable hair (Randall, 1969).

SUMMARY

The precise role of surgery in treatment of transsexuals is still unproven (Edgerton, 1974). Many reports have appeared with encouraging results, but the consistently unsuccessful results of all alternative nonsurgical methods of treating the male transsexual are strong arguments for careful continued study of the surgical treatments of these most needy patients (Benjamin, 1968; Edgerton, 1973; Edgerton and Meyer, 1973). The sincere and dedicated gender team should be involved in the assessment of the transsexual, and the procedure and follow-up should only be undertaken for scientific and humanistic reasons. Emotional needs and support are as essential as the surgical procedure itself.

Vaginoplasty in the male transsexual is directed not only at creating the external genitalia of a normal female but, more importantly, at producing adequate depth for intercourse and a normally placed urethral meatus to allow micturition to take place in the sitting position.

A review of the principles in the selection of patients for surgery, choice and timing of operations, comparisons of techniques and a general review of the results and complications of surgery has been presented.

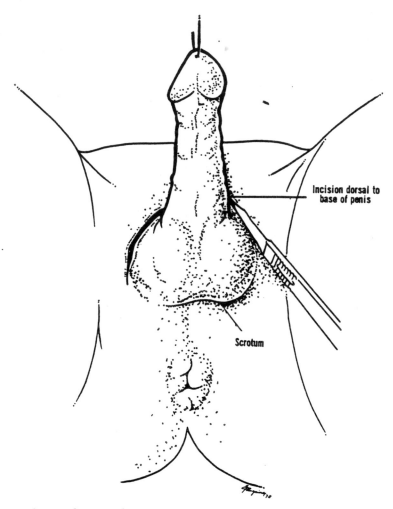

Incision dorsal to
base of penis

Scrotum

Figure 8-1. The initial incision is a U-shaped incision, curving around
the ventral surface of the base of the phallus. The posterior attachment
of the scrotum to the perineum constitutes the blood supply for the entire
vaginal flap.

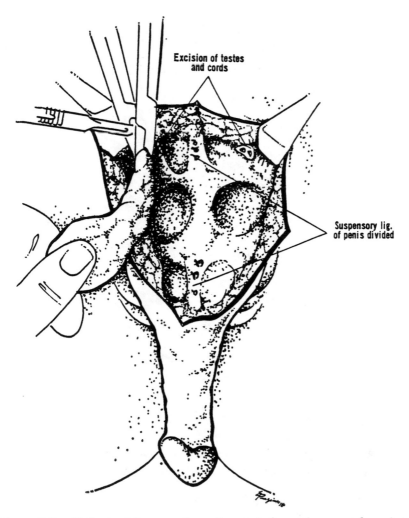

Excision of testes and cords

Suspensory lig. of penis divided

Figure 8-2. Both testicles are then dissected from the scrotal pockets, and the cord is freed on either side up to a point above the pubis. Here the vessels and vas are ligated on either side.

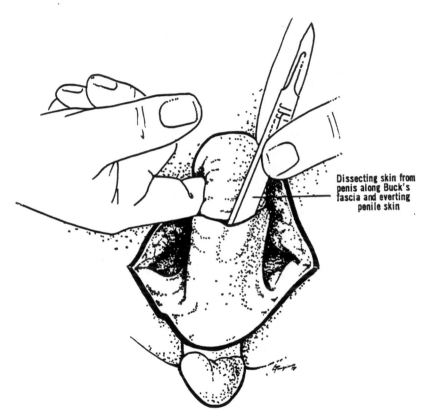

Dissecting skin from penis along Buck's fascia and everting penile skin

Figure 8-3. The shaft of the penis is then elevated with the finger, and a combination of sharp and blunt dissection along Buck's fascia will free the penile skin in a tubular fashion.

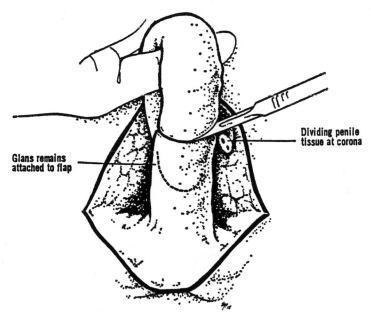

Dividing penile tissue at corona

Glans remains attached to flap

Figure 8-4. When the tip of the penis is reached, it is transsected so as to leave some of the deep glans attached to the skin. This tissue may later simulate a small cervix at the vault of the new vagina.

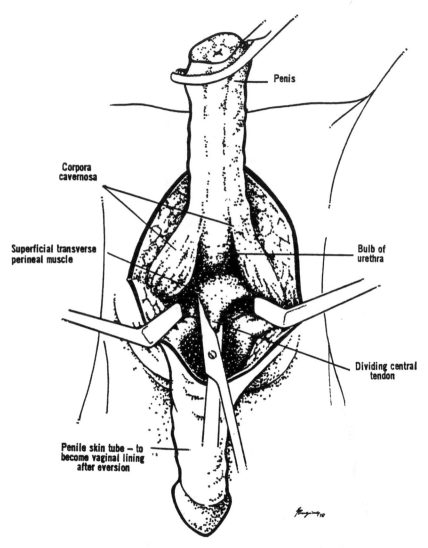

Figure 8-5. The central tendon of the perineum is divided in order to begin dissection along a plane between the prostate and the rectum. This pocket is at least 2.25 in. posterior to the base of the shaft of the penis.

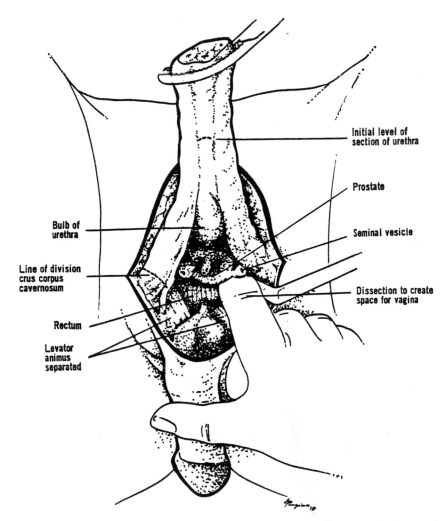

Figure 8-6. The dissection is carried out between the central fibers of the levator ani muscles and close to the posterior capsule of the small prostate. The seminal vesicles are identified, and the dissection is carried up to the reflection of the pelvic peritoneum.

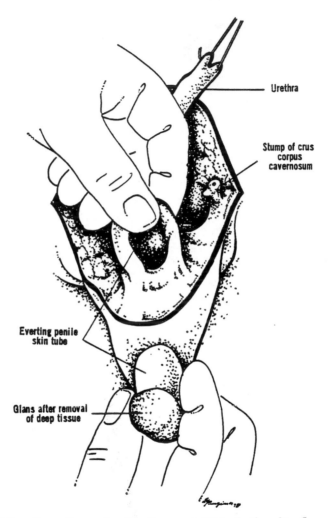

Urethra

Stump of crus
corpus
cavernosum

Everting penile
skin tube

Glans after removal
of deep tissue

Figure 8-7. Once the pocket has been established, the skin flap of penile skin is turned inside out and fitted up to the floor of the pelvis.

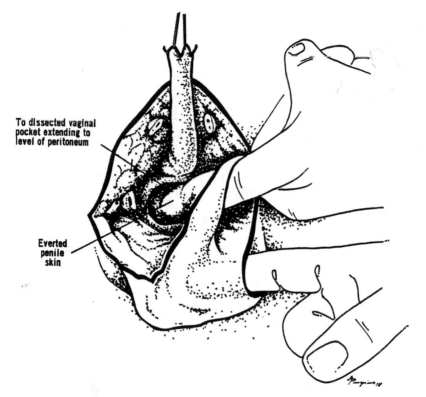

To dissected vaginal pocket extending to level of peritoneum

Everted penile skin

Figure 8-8. The urethra has been left intentionally long at this stage of the operation.

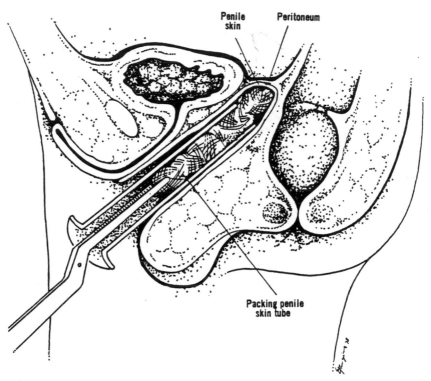

Figure 8-9. A coronal section of the newly created vagina. Packing is gently inserted with an anoscope to maintain full length and diameter of the vagina.

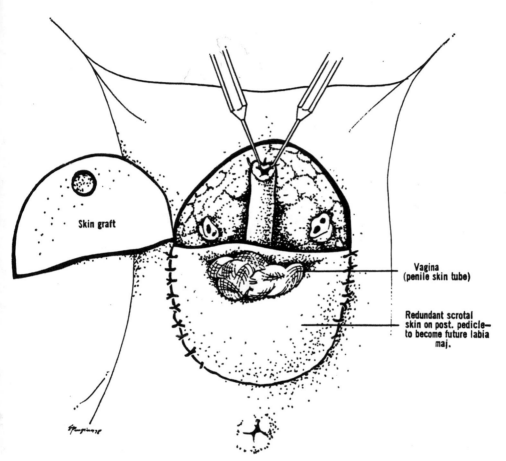

Skin graft

Vagina
(penile skin tube)

Redundant scrotal
skin on post. pedicle—
to become future labia
maj.

Figure 8-10.   The circulation of the skin flap is then checked with a light while the flap is in the position of the vagina. Redundant scrotal tissue forming the pedicle is left posteriorly, and a simple split-thickness skin graft is dressed anteriorly to cover the urethral stump and soft tissue defect.

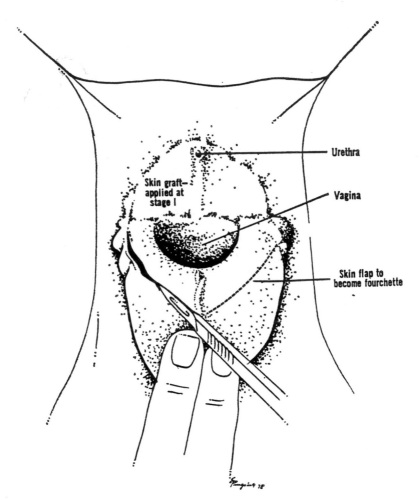

Figure 8-11. A triangular posterior skin flap of scrotal tissue is left attached to the rim of the vagina by the V-shaped incision. This prevents later constriction of the introitus.

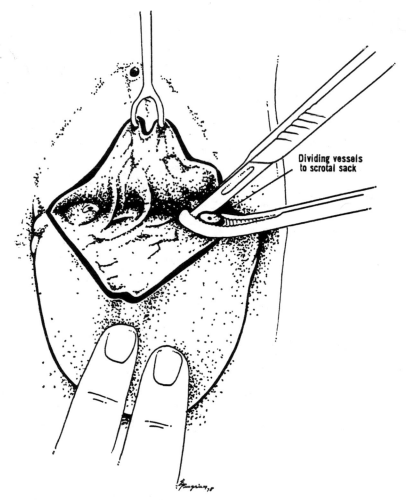

Figure 8-12. The superficial perineal arteries are divided on either side and ligated, and the remainder of the scrotal pedicle is divided in the midline back to a point 1 in. anterior to the anal canal.

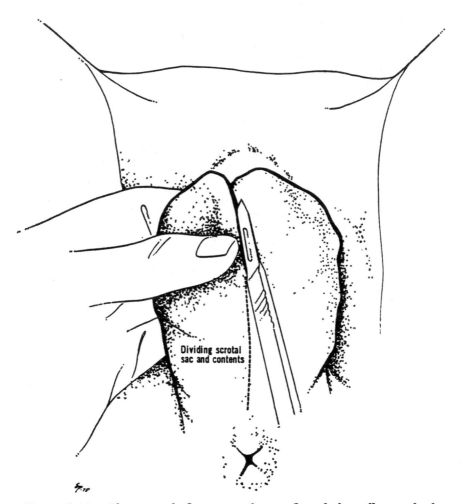

Dividing scrotal
sac and contents

Figure 8-13. The scrotal flaps are then reflected laterally, and the edematous tissue is removed from the undersurface. If desired, some of the tissue may be left in place and used in the construction of the labia.

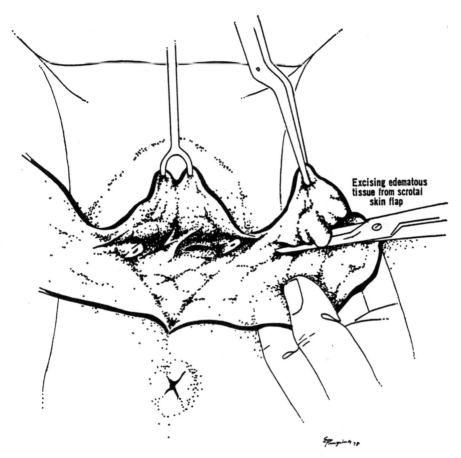

Excising edematous
tissue from scrotal
skin flap

Figure 8-14.

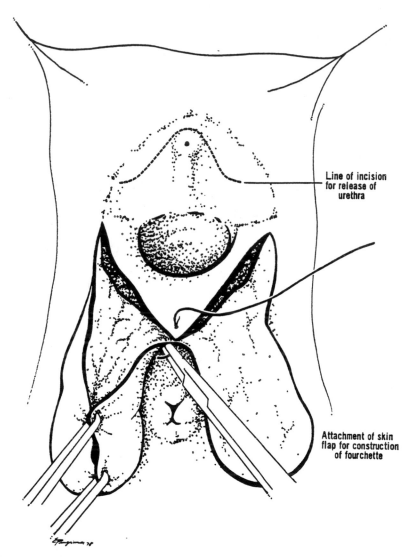

Figure 8-15. The posterior margin of the vagina is brought backward and attached appropriately to the midline anterior to the rectum, and the urethra is released anteriorly by a bell-shaped incision in the healed skin graft.

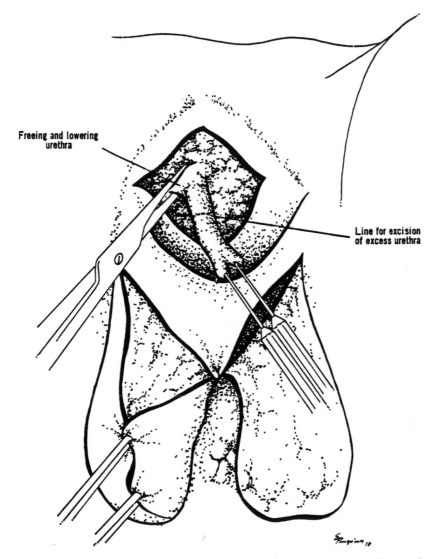

Freeing and lowering
urethra

Line for excision
of excess urethra

Figure 8-16. The overly long urethral stump is freed so that all erectile tissue can be removed, and the urethra is shortened to the level of the pubic rami.

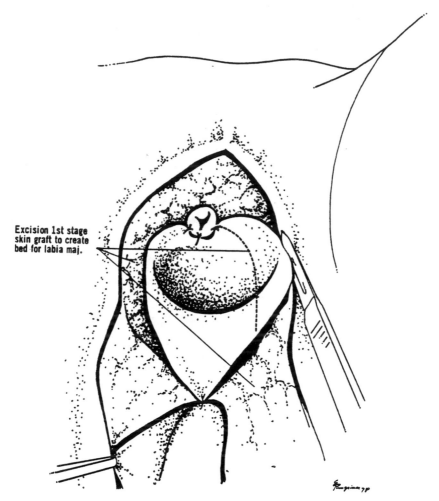

Excision 1st stage skin graft to create bed for labia maj.

Figure 8-17. At this point it is attached to the anterior vaginal wall, and the scrotal flaps are then fitted on either side of the vagina to create labia.

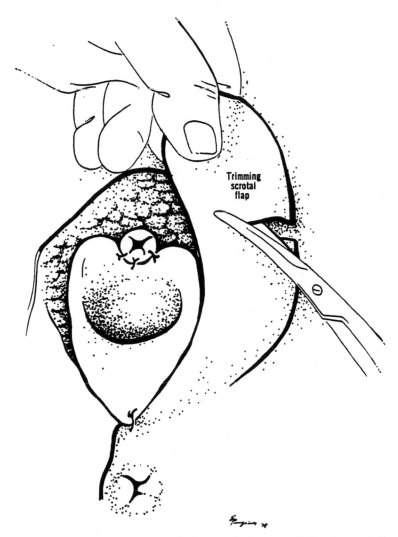

Figure 8-18. Final trimming and fitting of the scrotal flap is carried out so that, if desired, a small clitoral structure may be formed anteriorly—or simple folds on either side of the vagina may be created.

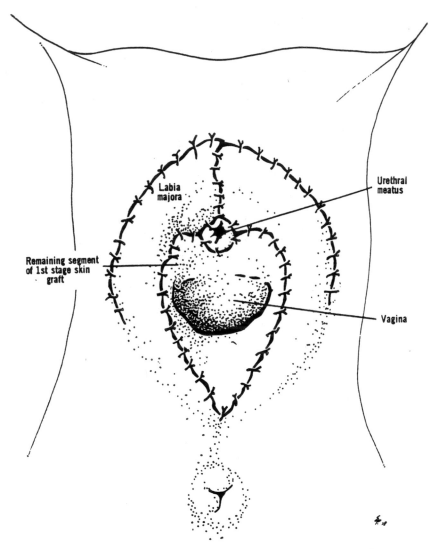

Figure 8-19. The scrotal flap has been trimmed to create the labial folds. The remaining flap of the first-stage graft is sutured inferiorly to the urethra and anteriorly to the vagina.

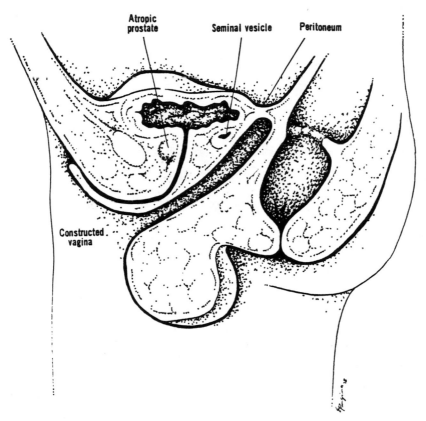

Figure 8-20. A coronal section of the neovagina demonstrating adequate depth of the vagina. The close relationship of the urethra and bladder is also demonstrated.

CHAPTER 8

CONCLUSION

T RANSSEXUALISM, A DESIRE to be the opposite sex; transvestism, an erotic pleasure in crossdressing; and homosexuality, an attraction to the same sex, have been accurately defined in the previous chapters. The clinically clearly delineated and easily separable cases of these three conditions are the ones that remain in the majority. However, these neatly packaged definitions often collapse, particularly when applied to cases having overlapping characteristics. Therefore, some of these cases are more accurately regarded as manifestations of a spectrum of disorders that defy unambiguous distinction. This spectrum of disorders is termed *gender dysphoria,* meaning a maladaptive displeasure over one's anatomical sex that drives the patient to desperate single-minded preoccupations with sex change. Gender dysphorias are found mostly in true transsexuals but also in some transvestites and effeminate homosexuals.

The presumed causes of these disorders or conditions have been discussed at length, but no ultimate answer has been found. Biological theories have been pitted against psychological etiologies, none of which seems capable of independently providing an all-embracing, universal explanation. Each of these insights is seemingly countered by contradictory data, although each has its own depth and segmental validity. Thus, it is evident that polarized biological and psychological concepts, as in other areas of human behavior, when viewed in isolation, are by themselves inadequate in providing "the answer." Partial answers, a more modest, realistic goal, are likely attainable when all fragments of knowledge are integrated. Old-fashioned bellicose partisanism between different schools of psychiatry is rapidly coming to a none-too-premature end. Likewise, outdated and labelistic terminology, riddled with ambiguities and far-fetched pseudo-scientism, demands a sincere review. Such a review can be done only if the presumed clinical "entities" are broken down into relevant subgroups of different etiologies and are studied separately. In currently used terminology, the psychological and physical-organic factors jointly appear to play proportionate roles in the etiology of transsexualism. The physical-organic factors, if present, are the most varied kinds of clinical or subclinical disorders.

Every clinical case, because of its complexity, requires responsible multidisciplinary exploration. Not unlike in Stoller's (1973) gender clinic, the psychiatric label is not necessarily a relevant issue. Instead, a patient's motivation, perseverance, general mental state, coping mechanisms, constellation of ego defenses and other prognostic factors (Stone, 1977) are the vital determinants to be examined before tragic, irreversible surgery is performed on those whose desire for sex change is merely transitory (Newman et al., 1974) or those who, after being sexually transformed to a female, wish to be changed back to the male status (Money, 1973). Nor can the physical aspect of the evaluation be too strongly emphasized.

Careful case study will likely provide sufficient indications as to the correct mode of treatment. Such study can be done only in a well-organized setting and with readily available teamwork. Of extreme importance is the careful consideration of the exclusion criteria for recommending surgery.

Surgery, so fervently desired by transsexuals, should currently be considered an effective, palliative, symptomatic treatment in well-selected cases, particularly because other treatment modalities are not really available. Psychological treatment forms, be they analytical or behavioral in orientation, are effective therapeutic tools in many other instances but fail as a rule with transsexuals, who are rarely, if ever, interested in what these treatments can offer. Furthermore, the technical difficulties of treatment and the unalterable nature of the condition have discouraged psychotherapists and have thus engendered a therapeutic pessimism from Freud to Money. Although scattered results of an insignificant number of cases are reported occasionally, the few patients with whom these approaches are successful represent a self-selected subgroup, remote from the typical cases.

The vast majority of transsexuals welcome the sex-change operation. Lothstein (1978) pointed out the frequent euphoria and flagrant lack of fear in these patients during the immediate preoperative period.

The sex-change operation is certainly not cosmetic surgery (Koranyi, 1976)—the denial of it can lead to suicide or self-castration. Quite apart from such grim mishaps, the denial of any medical procedure capable of providing significant relief and a better adaptation to the patient cannot be considered ethical. Because transsexualism has been known since ancient times, occasionally the argument is raised, "What did transsexuals do before modern surgery finally offered a new solution to them?" What they did is irrelevant, since no other disorder, apart from the common cold, is treated in modern times by ancient means. Surgery is now the available tool. However, its use is often limited by the emotionalism of some physicians (Green, 1966-67). What the future may bring in terms of the treatment and prevention of these disorders remains an open question.

Follow-up patient care before and after the operation, success of the surgical technique (Markland, 1973; Block and Tessler, 1971), the patient's social rehabilitation and the resolution of legal problems are of considerable importance in the attainment of improved overall adaptation. A transient period of exuberant promiscuity sometimes occurs after surgery, and is indicative of a need to be recognized in the new role.

The transsexual patient deserves to be treated with dignity by the medical and legal authorities. While the author has heard no complaints from his patients concerning doctors or lawyers in this respect, the same, unfortunately, cannot be stated of some of the police forces. Similar abuses are probably among the reasons why in France, where a 1907 law forbids men to wear skirts except during Mardi Gras, transsexuals have organized a union (*The Gazette*, Montreal, 1973) under the leadership of Marie Andre, a person whose appearance changed after German doctors in World War II experimentally administered female hormones to him.

Help, information and literature on various aspects of the daily problems of transsexuals and their relatives is readily available from some North American organizations, such as the Janus Society. Nor is there a shortage of scientific interest in the subject; reports on all aspects of transsexualism are presented regularly. Recent publications on the sometimes evident genetic abnormalities (McKee, 1976; Buhrich et al., 1978), the hormonal status (Davidson, 1977; Lenton et al., 1977; Halbreich et al., 1978) and neurological alterations (Lundberg et al., 1975; Nusselt et al., 1976; Kockott et al., 1976) have greatly added to the psychopathological observations (Franzini, 1977; Barr, 1976; Levine, 1976; Money, 1976; Langevin, 1977; Derogatis, 1978). Explorations of the different subtypes have now begun (Person, 1974; Buhrich, 1978), and carefully researched review articles (Ploeger, 1976) are extremely helpful in summing up rapidly expanding knowledge.

A final note concerns the importance of sexuality in human relationships in general. Prevalence studies of various sexual dysfunctions in the nonpsychiatric population (Levine and Yost, 1976; Frank et al., 1978) have proven that these conditions are indeed remarkably common. Not all "sexual dysfunctions" need to be attacked with a single-minded therapeutic zeal. These statistics prove that it is the totality of the human relation that counts (Koranyi, 1978). The quality of marital and human happiness and relationships does not hinge upon sexual craftsmanship. Most happily married and emotionally mature couples realize this fact. However, this is not so with many, if not most, homosexual or transsexual relationships, which are deeply perturbed by exclusive sexual preoccupations, jealousies and the need of the individuals to prove themselves.

Scientific insight into these disorders and conditions, into sexuality in general and into all other aspects of human behavior is now on the threshold of a new era. What a pity that progress at this stage is once again rendered stagnant by severely limited research funds.

GLOSSARY

ACTH. *See* adrenocorticotropic hormone.

ADRENAL GLAND. A small pyramidal-shaped pair of glandular organs positioned over each kidney in both sexes. Vitally important hormones are produced in them with the help of locally present enzymes. The outer, cortical part of the gland secretes hormones involved in the production of glucose (cortisol), mineral (aldosterone) metabolism and sexual steroid hormones, which influence sexual development and sexual functioning. Both the male and female produce male-type hormones in these glands. All these hormones are under the regulatory control of certain brain parts via the pituitary gland. The innermost, medullary part of the adrenal gland secretes adrenaline, a substance required for quick adaptive responses.

ADRENOCORTICAL. Refers to the outer, cortical part of the adrenal gland, as distinguished from the inner, medullary part.

ADRENOCORTICOTROPIC HORMONE. ACTH, one of the hormones produced in the pituitary gland. ACTH raises and regulates the function of the cortical part of the adrenal gland. Brain-bound (hypothalamic) sensors elevate the levels of ACTH if the adrenocortical gland happens to be underfunctioning in relation to the momentary need.

ADRENOGENITAL SYNDROME. A collection of characteristic physical and psychological symptoms caused by a defect in the cortical part of the adrenal gland, with consequent overfunctioning of this organ. Adult onset forms ensue as a result of hormone-producing tumors or other pathologies. Hereditary forms exist due to absolute or relative deficiency of local enzymes with faulty biosynthesis (too little cortisol, too much sex steroids). Similar states ensue upon administration of certain kinds of hormones to the pregnant mother or due to other teratogenic causes. The most pronounced result of the disorder is in the female fetus, which will show virilized genitalia

161

and psychological virilization. In the incomplete form of this pathology, physical malformations may be absent or minimal, but psychological, behavioral virilization will prevail.

ALDOSTERONE. One of the adrenocortical hormones having an impact on the mineral metabolism and blood pressure.

AMYGDALA. The amygdala, or amygdaloid complex, is a brain part belonging to the limbic system and is located in the tip of the temporal lobe of the brain. The function of the amygdala includes the provision of a flow of motivational energy directed towards basic needs and instincts. These energies are harnessed in the process of biological adaptation. Disorders of the amygdala result in aggressive behavior, hyper- or hyposexuality, bizarre sexuality and other behavioral deviations. In rare instances, transvestism has been observed with a variety of amygdala-temporal lobe abnormalities.

ANACLITIC DEPRESSION. Severe depression developing in some infants upon separation from the mother.

ANDROGENS. Hormones or other chemicals with masculinizing properties.

ANTIANDROGEN. Chemical substance that cancels the action of male sexual hormones.

ANTICONVULSANTS. Antiepileptic medications or substances.

APHRODISIAC. Any drug or substance that causes sexual excitement, elevates sexual desire or is believed to improve sexual performance.

AUTOEROTICISM. Masturbation.

AUTONOMIC NERVOUS SYSTEM. Part of the central (brain) and peripheral nervous system that is responsible for self-regulating body functions. The autonomous nervous system is relatively independent and uninfluenced by volition but is strongly affected by emotions. *See also* hypothalamus.

AUTOSOMES. Of the forty-six human chromosomes, forty-four are autosomes, which are involved in the transmission of other than sex-determining tasks in the normal human. *See also* chromosomes, sex chromosomes.

BARR BODY. Also called sex chromatin, Barr bodies are dark-staining small dots, present in all normal female cells, best seen at particular phases of cellular division (interphase). The sex chromatin represents an inactivated X chromosome.

Barr bodies are normally absent in the male. No change of Barr bodies occurs after transsexual surgery. *See also* nuclear sex.

BISEXUALITY. (1) Presence of degrees of male and female biological characteristics in animal or human organisms. *See also* dimorphism, psychic hermaphroditism. (2) Capacity for being sexually attracted to and active with both sexes.

BRANCHIAL ARCH. Remnants of gills in the human.

CHROMOSOMAL SEX. Sex of the offspring is determined at the moment of conception: the normal female sex chromosome constellation is XX and the normal male is XY. Maleness of the offspring is determined by the Y chromosome. Abnormalities: XX male and XY female exist, and numerically abnormal sex chromosomes (Turner's syndrome, Klinefelter's syndrome) occur with typical consequences. *See also* chromosomes, Turner's syndrome, Klinefelter's syndrome.

CHROMOSOMES. Hereditary particles situated in the nucleus of all cells. They are dark-staining threadlike structures consisting of the giant molecule DNA and protein. The molecular peculiarities of DNA (unique sequences of sugar, base and nucleic acid) harbor the genetic information. The number of human chromosomes is 46, of which 44 are autosomes and 2 are sex chromosomes.

CLITORIS. Small erectile tissue, partially covered by a hood, above the anterior edge of the vaginal opening and the urethra, where the two minor labia meet. The clitoris is a developmental analogue of the penis.

CONDITIONED REFLEX. An associational tie between an unconditioned pleasure and the environmental circumstances or conditions under which such pleasure takes place. *See also* limbic system.

CORE GENDER IDENTITY. Very early psychological recognition of belonging to one or the other sex. This step occurs before eighteen months of age. It is disturbed in transsexuals, who are said to acquire a cross gender identity, but is usually not disturbed in homosexuals or in transvestites.

CORPORA CAVERNOSA. Erectile tissue in the penis.

CORTEX. External coverage, rind. If not otherwise specified, the outer, convoluted coverage of gray matter enveloping the brain with this cellular layer of nerve cells. *Adrenal cortex* refers to the outer layer of the adrenal gland.

CORTISOL. One of the adrenocortical hormones having an impact on the glucose metabolism and many other functions.

CRITICAL PHASE OF DEVELOPMENT. A preset chain of biological events from conception to maturity that must take place within a rigidly defined timetable. Similar critical phases of psychological and physiological stages were postulated from birth to maturity.

CROSS GENDER IDENTITY. *See* core gender identity.

CROSSDRESSING. The act of wearing the garments of the opposite sex. In transsexuals, the desire to crossdress has an early onset and is not accompanied by sexual excitement but represents a consuming desire in which transsexuals report that they feel peaceful and natural. In transvestism, crossdressing is usually episodic and is accompanied by sexual excitement. Effeminate homosexuals crossdress occasionally. Female impersonators represent a different category.

CYPROTERONE ACETATE. *See* antiandrogen.

DNA. Desoxyribonucleic acid, a substance present in the cell nucleus and containing genetic information. *See also* chromosomes.

DEMENTIA. Loss of intellectual capacity determined by organic pathological processes. It is accompanied by a decline of judgment and memory. *See also* organic brain syndrome, presenile dementia.

DIMORPHISM. (1) Appearing in two forms; the characteristic of a species having male and female forms. (2) The fact that parallel to the dominantly male or respective female features everyone shares an overlap with the opposite sex. The dimorphism is not entirely complete in any of the species because of this overlap. *See also* psychic hermaphroditism, bisexuality.

DIPLOID. Chromosomes are present in pairs within the cell nucleus. This condition is referred to as diploid. Before conception can take place, the germ cells (sperm and ovum) undergo a complex cellular division and lose half of their chromosomes; the cell assumes a haploid form so that when the sperm and ovum unite, the offspring will have a total chromosomal number of 46 and be restored to a diploid state. *See also* haploid, meiosis, nondisjunction.

DOMINANT INHERITANCE. The hereditary transmission of a parental gene (trait) of which the parent is a carrier (heterozygote) and the manifestation of which appears in the offspring.

DOWN'S SYNDROME. A chromosomal disorder with a supernumerary chromosome (trisomy) in the twenty-first pair, resulting in mongolism with mental subnormality and physical characteristics.

DYSFUNCTION. Disturbed or abnormal function.

DYSPHORIA. Displeasure, anguish, altered mood.

EGO. "Self," as one appears to him/herself or to others. Ego is part of Freud's "psychic apparatus" (mind). According to the divisions of his structural theory, the Ego is a mediating agency of the mind, guided by the "reality principle." The Ego brings about a behavioral compromise between the Id (primitive urges) and the Superego (conscience). *See also* Id, Superego, psychosexual development.

ENZYME. A protein type of substance that facilitates or causes a specific chemical transformation in other substances. Enzymes are also involved in the production of hormones.

ÉONISM. Old name for transsexualism-transvestism deriving from the famous eighteenth-century crossdresser Chevalier Éon de Beaumont.

ESTROGEN. Feminizing (estrus-producing) hormones or substances. The most important estrogen is estradiol, secreted by the ovary, where it is produced from androgenic (testosterone) precursors.

EXHIBITIONISM. Sexual gratification derived from causing sexual response (approval or disapproval) in others by degrees of self-exposure within a particular cultural setting.

EXTERNAL GENITALIA. The visible parts of male and female genitalia.

FISTULA. Unnatural opening or communication via a pathological opening.

FSH. Follicle-stimulating hormone, a pituitary gland product, present in both sexes and active in the fetus, where it is responsible for the normal development of the sexual organs. In early teens, this hormone contributes to the evolution of secondary sex characteristics.

FSH-RH. Follicle-stimulating-hormone-releasing hormone, a hypothalamic brain hormone that stimulates the production and release of FSH.

FETISHISM. A condition characterized by sexual excitation displaced from a person to an inanimate object (e.g. from a female person to female undergarments). Also, adoration or love of an inanimate object.

FIXATION. Impediment along the line of development. *See also* psychosexual development.

FOLLICLE-STIMULATING HORMONE. *See* FSH.

FRIGIDITY. Absence of female orgasm. Determined by psychological or physical causes.

GnRH. Gonadrotropin-releasing hormone (FSH-RH and LH-RH). Hypothalamic hormones that are responsible for the production of FSH and LH in the pituitary gland and thus indirectly influence the testes and ovaries.

GAMETES. Germ cells: sperm and ovum.

GENES. Self-reproducing hereditary units consisting of part of the DNA molecule and responsible for the production of peptides. The genes are located at specific sites on the chromosomes and transmit latent or manifest traits from one generation to the next. *See also* heterozygote, homozygote.

GENDER. Male or female forms of the same species.

GENDER DYSPHORIA. Displeasure, anguish over one's anatomical sexual belonging with a hateful attitude toward one's sexual organ. Maladaptation to one's morphological sexuality and wishing to become the opposite sex. It is present mostly in transsexuals, but the same may ocur in some transvestites and effeminate homosexuals.

GENDER IDENTITY. *See* core gender identity.

GENETIC CODE. Particular sequences of chemicals (sugar, base, nucleic acid) within the DNA molecule, containing and reproducing hereditary information.

GENOTYPE. The constitution or makeup of an individual as

determined by the collection of his/her genes. Not all genes come to a manifest expression. *See also* phenotype.

GONAD. Common name for male testis and the female ovary, that is, organs that create germ cells. Male/female reproductive organs.

GONADAL DYSGENESIS. Congenital failure to develop reproductive organs (testes and ovaries).

GONADAL SEX. Sex as defined by the gonadal (testis, ovary) tissues present in an individual. In cases of true hermaphroditism, both tissues are present with a predilection to develop into malignant tumors.

GONADOTROPIN-RELEASING HORMONE. *See* GnRH.

GRAY MATTER; CORTICAL, SUBCORTICAL. Cellular parts of the brain tissue located on the surface (cortex) or in the depth of the brain (subcortical nuclei). *See also* cortex.

GYNECOMASTIA. Excess development of the male mammary gland.

H-Y ANTIGEN. Chemical substance located in the long arm of the Y chromosome, presumed to determine the male sex of the offspring.

HAPLOID. *See* diploid, meiosis.

HERMAPHRODITISM. Sexual ambiguity whereby an organism exhibits anatomical or psychological features of both sexes. *See also* true hermaphroditism, pseudohermaphroditism, adrenogenital syndrome.

HETEROZYGOTE. Differing genes (one maternal, one paternal) in the same chromosomal location, rendering such a person the carrier of either parental trends. *See also* homozygote, chromosomes, genes.

HIPPOCAMPUS. Brain part in the temporal lobe related to memory processes. *See also* limbic system.

HIRSUTISM. Abnormal hair growth.

HOMOSEXUALITY. Sexual and emotional attraction to the same sex. Widespread in all species.

HOMOZYGOTE. Two identical genes on the corresponding chromosomes at the identical location. *See also* heterozygote, chromosomes, gene.

HORMONE. Chemical substance produced in various glands,

secreted into the bloodstream, reaching the target organ in that way and bringing about specific responses through special receptors.

HORMONAL SEX. Both male and female hormones are present in both sexes, but the level of male hormones is much higher in men and the level of female hormones much higher in women. The quantitative profile of the sex hormones is characteristic to normally sexed men and women.

HYPOGLYCEMIA. Low levels of blood sugar from whatever causes.

HYPOGONADISM. Decreased function of the gonads resulting in sexual underdevelopment.

HYPOSEXUALITY. Decreased sexual drive.

HYPOTHALAMUS. Brain part concerned with autonomic, metabolic hormonal responses and attunement of the body for a particular task ahead. It also produces hormones that stimulate the pituitary gland. A multitude of different receptors of the hypothalamus continually monitor the blood composition in order to initiate corrective measures and maintain normal chemical balance. Hypothalamic functions also include hormonal influences on sexual development, sexual interest, female cyclicity and secondary sexual characteristics. Closely interrelated with the limbic system.

ID. Part of the mind that motivates primitive, crude, animallike behavior, energized by the instincts. It strives for immediate gratification (pleasure principle). The Id counterbalances the Ego and Superego. The Id can be tentatively identified with the brain part of the limbic system. *See also* amygdala, limbic system, Ego, Superego, libido.

IDENTIFICATION. Psychoanalytic concept of accepting, "introjecting" and becoming similar to aspects of an important person, usually a parent. The process of identification takes place in early childhood.

IMPOTENCE. Inability to produce or to maintain penile erection due to psychological causes, or because of a variety of physical illnesses, drug and alcohol abuse or side effects of certain medications.

IMPRINT. The biological retention of an external image or

event taking place in early life and having an indelible influence upon behavior.

INDIFFERENT GONAD. The earliest stage of development of the genital organs in the embryo, with the potential to evolve into either male or female. If not otherwise influenced, all indifferent gonads, and thus all offspring, become females. The presumed substance determining male development is the H-Y antigen, located in the long arm of the Y chromosome.

INSTINCT. Biological energy or drive, retained for a particular basic behavior.

INTERNAL GENITALIA. Uterus, ovaries, Fallopian tubes in the female; glands, ducts in both sexes; prostate in the male.

KARYOTYPING. Technique for staining and photographing the chromosomes.

KLINEFELTER'S SYNDROME. Supernumerary X chromosome in the human male showing 47XXY instead of the normal 46XY chromosomes. Hypogonadism, hyposexuality, gynecomastia and low levels of male sex hormones with elevated levels of female sex hormones account for impotence or frequent regressive or aberrant sexuality.

KLUVER-BUCY OPERATION. Originally research done on monkeys that involved cutting the tip of the temporal lobe. This surgery resulted in reduced aggression, increased sexuality, bizarre sexuality and abnormal appetite and food intake among other symptoms.

LH. Luteinizing hormone, a pituitary gland hormone present in both sexes and already active in the fetus. Promotes the formation of testosterone and progesterone. In collaboration with FSH, luteinizing hormone brings about the evolvement of secondary sexual characteristics. It also acts as an aphrodisiac.

LH-RH. Luteinizing-hormone-releasing hormone, a hypothalamic chemical substance that stimulates the release of LH in the pituitary gland.

LABIA. Tissue folds embracing the vagina. The major labia represents the outer and the minor labia the inner folds.

LABIOSCROTAL FUSION. A congenital abnormality in the female, consisting of a closure of the vaginal labia, expressing a masculinizing influence upon the female embryo.

LARYNGEAL. Pertinent to the larynx, the vocal cord and vocal apparatus.

LATENT HOMOSEXUALITY. Homosexuality that is presumed to be denied and deleted from the conscious mind but continues to exist in a repressed form.

LEYDIG CELLS. Testosterone-producing cells in the testes. There are two families of Leydig cells, the first being active in the embryo, the other becoming active in puberty.

LIBIDO. Sexual drive.

LIMBIC SYSTEM. Brain part related to the task of biological adaptation and survival. The limbic system also contains the motivational drive (amygdala), the nose brain (olfactory areas), the reward system (septal nuclei) and the memory functions (hippocampus). The limbic system, a structure common to all mammals, is regarded as the site where basic crude emotions and impulses are generated. With approximation, it corresponds to the psychoanalytic concept of Id.

LINKAGE MAP. Chromosomes come in pairs. The corresponding chromosome in the pair is referred to as being homologous. Different genes carrying different traits and occupying the same location on the homologous chromosomes are linked. This linkage permits the design of a genetic map concerning the chromosomes.

LUTEINIZING HORMONE. *See* LH.

MAMILLARY BODIES. A pair of small organs on the base of the brain belonging to the hypothalamus, closely related to the limbic system. Among others, they relate to memory functions.

MASOCHISM. Converting the experience of pain or humiliation into sexual excitation. Also, indulgence in self-torture. Masochism can exist from mild to severe forms. It is the mirror-image opposite of sadism, the two being interrelated and often referred to as sadomasochism, as it is presumed that both features are present in slight degrees in everyone. It is believed that slight masochism prevails in women and slight sadism in men.

MEIOSIS. Complex cell division occurring in the gametes (sperm, ovum). *See also* diploid.

MEMORY. Ability to retain, code, store and retrieve earlier events important to the adaptive behavior through biochemical and electrophysiological processes. Memory is akin to learning and is part of general intelligence. Subserving biological adaptation, memory relates to the limbic system.

MOSAICISM. Presence of different chromosomal lines within the same tissue, e.g. XX as well as XY cells in cases of true hermaphroditism.

MUTATION. A change in the genes or in the chromosomes occurring either spontaneously or induced by teratogenic influences. If mutation involves the gametes (sperm, ovum), the emerging new characteristics are transmitted to the offspring.

NEOCORTEX. *See* cortex.

NEURON. Unit of the nervous system, the nerve cell with its connections and processes.

NONDISJUNCTION. Failure of the germ cell to pass from diploid to haploid state. *See also* diploid.

NUCLEAR SEX. In normal females, one "superfluous" X chromosome becomes inactivated, and it shows up under microscopic examination as a dark-stained dot near the wall of the cell nucleus. This dot is also called sex chromatin or Barr body. *See also* Barr body, chromatin.

NUCLEUS. Round body within the cell containing the chromosomes and other distinct structures.

OLFACTORY TRACT. The first cranial nerve, relating to the sense of smell. It connects with certain primitive brain areas belonging to the limbic system. *See also* limbic system.

OOCYTE. Developing, not yet mature ovum, or egg cell.

ORGANIC BRAIN SYNDROME. Collection of symptoms characteristic to transient or permanent localized or generalized damage to the brain.

OVARIAN FOLLICLES. The site of the egg cell in the ovary, the ovum and its coverage.

OVARY. Female sexual gland where male and female sexual hormones and the ova are produced. Anatomical analogue of the male testis.

OVUM. Egg cell, produced in the ovary.

PAROXYSMAL DISORDER. Periodically occurring involuntary seizures and all forms of epilepsies. Periodic poorly motivated aggressive or altered sexual behavior may also occur in some forms with epilepsies. Abnormal electrical discharges within the brain.

PEDOPHILIA. Sexual attraction and sexual act on the part of an adult person involving children.

PEPTIDES. Organic chemical substances containing small numbers of amino acids. They act as mediators in the brain.

PERVERSION. Sexual deviations of all kinds.

PHENOTYPE. The totality of an individual's physical, biochemical makeup resulting from his/her genetic endowment (genotype) as it is modified by the environment. *See also* genotype.

PHEROMONES. Trace chemicals present in many kinds of excreta (sweat, milk, urine, etc.) of a human or animal organism capable of transmitting his/her characteristics to other members of the species through smell.

PHYLOGENY. Biological developmental history of the species.

PITUITARY. Or hypophysis; a small gland located in the base of the brain, connected with and regulated by the brain part called hypothalamus. The pituitary gland regulates all other hormone systems of the body via its specific hormones.

PLASTICITY. The ability to change.

POLYMORPHOUS PERVERSE. Psychoanalytic term describing the infant's striving for satisfaction regardless of its source or nature. Thus, the infant is believed to possess a potential for all behaviors that in the adult world would be considered as perverted.

POSTNATAL. After birth.

PRESENILE DEMENTIA. Progressive, eventually fatal, distinct degenerative pathology of the brain of unknown etiology, occurring from the fourth decade of life onwards.

PROGESTERONE. Hormone formed from cholesterol (via pregnanolone), occupying a crucial point in the formation of three types of steroid hormones: aldosterone, cortisol and sex steroids (testosterone and estrogen synthesis).

PROLACTIN. Pituitary hormone affecting breast development, milk production and sexual functioning. Present and active in both sexes.

PSEUDOHERMAPHRODITISM. Male or female with ambiguous sexual morphology and frequently disturbed sexual role and sexual identity but with unambiguous gonads.

PSYCHIC HERMAPHRODITISM. (1) Normal state described in all humans expressing the proportionate maleness or femaleness shared by all. (2) Pathological condition describing a masculinization of the female or feminization of the male fetus, infant or child due to genetic or other means but without observable sexual malformation. *See also* adreno-genital syndrome.

PSYCHOSEXUAL DEVELOPMENT. Psychoanalytic term describing presumed stages of child development. The psychological energy of the sexual instinct (libido) is, according to this theory, sequentially repositioned from oral to anal and phallic regions and, subsequent to a latency period, finally to the genital region. Each of these stages is assumed to be associated with the acquisition of typical features. A developmental failure, fixation, is a possibility at any of these stages.

PSYCHOSIS. Insanity, gross break with reality.

RNA. Ribonucleic acid. This chemical substance, akin to DNA, is present in the cell nucleus and nucleolus and is involved in the process of transmitting genetic information and protein synthesis.

RECEPTOR. Specialized sensor.

RECESSIVE INHERITANCE. Heterozygotous genes that remain latent in the offspring. *See also* homozygote, heterozygote, dominant inheritance.

RECTOVAGINAL FISTULA. An unnatural opening between the vagina and the tissues behind the vagina.

REGRESSION. Temporary or permanent return to a lesser hierarchy of developmental stage, with manifestation of primitive behavior in all or selected areas of mental functioning.

RELEASING HORMONES. Hypothalamic hormones instigating the production and release of pituitary hormones.

RHINENCEPHALON. Brain areas connected with the sense of smell and with basic adaptive behavior. *See also* limbic system.

RHINOPLASTY. Operation to reshape the contour of the nose.

SADISM. *See* masochism

SADOMASOCHISM. *See* masochism.

SECONDARY SEX CHARACTERISTICS. Typical male or female features, which develop from early teens onwards. These include sexual differences in the voice, hair (scalp, facial, body, genital), breasts, subcutaneous fat distribution. *See also* FSH and LH.

SEPTAL NUCLEI. One of the brain areas that is connected with the experience of pleasure or reward. When the septal nuclei fire (electric discharge occurs), pleasure is experienced, causing the circumstances under which this pleasure took place to be registered in the memory and thus creating a further need for the same. The septal nuclei and other reward systems in the brain play vital roles in learning adaptive (or maladaptive) behavior.

SEX CHROMATIN. *See* Barr body.

SEX CHROMOSOMES. There are two sex chromosomes: the male pattern XY and the female pattern XX. The Y chromosome is involved in the determination of the maleness of the offspring.

SEXUAL DIMORPHISM. *See* dimorphism.

SEXUAL ROLE. Biologically, psychologically, developmentally and socially determined sexual behavior in the male and female.

SPERM. Male germ cells produced in the tubules of the testis.

SPERMATOZOA. Mature male germ cells.

STEROID HORMONES. Group of chemical substances deriving from cholesterol. They include sex steroids, cortisol, aldosterone. *See also* adrenal gland, progesterone, cholesterol.

SUPEREGO. *See* Id.

SUPRARENAL. Adrenal.

TEMPORAL LOBE. Part of the brain. *See also* limbic system.

TERATOGENIC. Having a propensity to derail embryonal development, leading to malformations.

TESTICULAR FEMINIZATION SYNDROME. A genetic male with 46XY chromosomes, high testosterone levels but absent or reduced sensitivity of the tissues to testosterone. The person develops along the female line, with female external genitalia, no internal genitalia and female secondary sex characteristics.

TESTIS. Testicle. Site of production of testosterone (in the Leydig cells) and sperm (in the tubules).

TESTOSTERONE. Male hormone produced in the adrenal glands, in the testes and ovaries. At the latter site and in the peripheral tissues it converts (is aromatized) into estrogen.

TRANSLOCATION. Gene accidentally transposed from a particular chromosome onto another.

TRANSSEXUALITY. In its pure clinical form, a psychological and sexual development corresponding to the opposite sex with a cross gender identity, including crossdressing from an early age onwards without sexual excitement. A continual and consuming desire to belong to the opposite sex is a characteristic feature, as is hatred or dislike of one's own genital organs. The sexual orientation in relation to the anatomical sexual organ is exclusively homosexual. *See also* gender dysphoria.

TRANSVESTISM. In its pure clinical form, this form of fetishism is typified by periodic crossdressing accompanied by sexual excitement. This is relieved by autoerotic means or by the services of specialized prostitutes. The usual sexual orientation is heterosexual, sometimes homosexual. *See also* fetishism, gender dysphoria.

TRISOMY. The presence of a third, instead of the usual two, chromosomes in a particular chromosomal pair. *See also* nondisjunction, Down's syndrome.

TRUE HERMAPHRODITISM. The presence of both male XY and female XX type of cells in the same tissue. In such a person, usually both testes and ovaries are present (ovotestis). *See also* gonadal sex.

TURNER'S SYNDROME. Female with only one X chromosome, resulting in gonadal dysgenesis and typical body build, physical and psychological sexual characteristics.

URETHRA. Canal with the function of conveying urine from the bladder to the external opening.

URETHROVAGINAL FISTULA. Pathological communication between the urethra and vagina.

X CHROMOSOMES. *See* sex chromosomes.

Y CHROMOSOMES. *See* sex chromosomes.

BIBLIOGRAPHY

Abraham, F.: Genitalumwandlung an zwei Mannlichen Transvestiten. Z *Sexualwiss, 18*:223-226, 1931.

In re Anonymous, 57 Misc. 2d, 813, 292 N.Y.S.2d 834 (N.Y. City Civ. Ct. 1968).

Anonymous v. Weiner, 50 Misc. 2d, 380, 270 N.Y.S. (Sup. Ct. 1966).

Bailyn, B., Davis, D.B., Donald, D.H., Thomas, J.L., Wiebe, R.H., and Wood, G.S.: *The Great Republic.* Boston, Little, 1977.

Baker, H.J.: Transsexualism—Problems in treatment. *Am J Psychiatry, 125*:123, 1969.

Baltzer, F.: Entwicklungsmechanische Untersuchungen an *Borellia viridis*, Teil III. *Publel Sta Zool Napoli, 16*:89, 1937.

Baram, T., Koch, Y., Hazum, E., and Fridkin, M.: Gonadotropin-releasing hormone in milk. *Science, 198*:300-301, 1977.

Barchas, J.D., Akil, H., Elliott, G.R., Holman, R.B., and Watson, S.J.: Behavioral neurochemistry: Neuroregulators and behavioral states. *Science, 200*:964-973, 1978.

Bard, P.: A diencephalic mechanism for the expression of rage with special reference to the sympathetic nervous system. *Am J Physiol, 84*:490-515, 1928.

Barr, R. and Blaszczynski, A.: Autonomic responses of transsexual and homosexual males to erotic film sequences. *Arch Sex Behav, 5(3):* 211-222, 1976.

Bartter, F.C., Forbes, A.P., and Lief, A.: Congenital adrenal hyperplasia associated with the adrenogenital syndrome: An attempt to correct its disordered hormonal pattern. *J Clin Invest, 29*:797, 1950.

Barwin, B.N.: Vaginoplasty—A simple approach to vaginal agenesis. In *Proceedings of Symposium on the Human Vagina and Health Disease.* Detroit, Michigan, Wayne State University, Oct. 28-30, 1976, p. 30.

Baum, M.J., Keverne, E.B., Everitt, B.J., Herbert, J., and DeGreef, W.J.: Effects of progesterone and estradiol on sexual attractivity of female rhesus monkeys. *Physiol Behav, 18*:659-670, 1977.

Beach, F.A.: Execution of the complete masculine copulatory pattern by sexually receptive female rats. *J Genet Psychol, 60*:137-142, 1942.

Beach, F.A.: Factors involved in the control of mounting behavior by female mammals. In Diamond, M. (Ed.): *Perspectives in Reproduction and Sexual Behavior.* Bloomington, Ind U P, 1968, pp. 83-131.

Becker, G.W.: *Der Rathgeber vor, bey und nach dem Beyschlafe.* Basel, bey Samuel Flick, 1807.

Belli, M.M.: Transsexual surgery. A new tort? *JAMA*, *239*:2143-2148, 1978.

Benjamin, H.: *The Transsexual Phenomenon*. New York, Julian, 1966.

Benjamin, H. and Masters, R.: A new kind of prostitute. *Sexology*, *30*: 446-448, 1964.

Benjamin, H. and Masters, R.: *Prostitution and Morality*. New York, Julian, 1964, p. 166.

Benjamin, H.: Transvestism and transsexualism in the male and female. *J Sex Res*, *3*:107, 1967.

Bennett, E.L., Diamond, M.C., Krech, D., and Rosenzweig, M.R.: Chemical and anatomical plasticity of brain. *Science*, *146*:610-619, 1964.

Bennett, E.L., Rosenzweig, M.R., and Wu, S.Y.C.: Excitant and depressant drugs modulate effects of environment on brain weight and cholinesterases. *Psychopharmacologia*, *33*:309-328, 1973.

Berkey v. Anderson, I.C.A.3d 790, 82 C.R. 67, 1970.

Bidlingmaier, F. and Knorr, D.: Inhibition of masculine differentiation in male offspring of rabbits actively immunised against testosterone before pregnancy. *Nature*, *266*:647-648, 1977.

Bieber, I.: *Homosexuality: A Psychological Study*. New York, Basic, 1962.

Bieber, I.: Sexuality, 1956-1976. *J Am Acad Psychoanal*, *5*(2):195-205, 1977.

Birk, L., Williams, G.H., Chasin, M., and Rose, L.I.: Serum testosterone levels in homosexual men. *N Engl J Med*, *289*:1236-1238, 1973.

Blackstone, W.: *Commentaries on the Laws of England*, vol. 4, sections 205-206. South Hackensack, N.J., Rothman Repr, 1803.

Block, N.L. and Tessler, A.N.: Transsexualism and surgical procedures. *Surg Gynecol Obstet*, March, 517-525, 1971.

Blumer, D.: Temporal lobe epilepsy and its psychiatric significance. In Benson, D.F. and Blumer, D. (Eds.): *Psychiatric Aspects of Neurological Disease*. New York, Grune, 1975, pp. 171-198.

Blumer, D. and Walker, A.E.: The neural basis of sexual behavior. In Benson, D.F. and Blumer, D. (Eds.): *Psychiatric Aspects of Neurological Disease*. New York, Grune, 1975, pp. 199-217.

Brown, B.B. and Fryer, M.P.: Plastic surgical correction of hypospadias with mistaken sex infertility and transvestism resulting in normal marriage and parenthood. *Surg Gynecol Obstet*, *118*:45-46, 1964.

Browne, J.S.L.: Discussion. In Ingele, D.J.: Hormones and metabolism, parameters of metabolic problems. *Recent Progr Horm Res*, *6*:159-194, 1951.

Buhrich, N., Barr, R. and Lam-Po-Tang, P.R.L.C.: Two transsexuals with 47-XYY karyotype. *Br J Psychiatry*, *133*:77-81, 1978.

Buhrich, N. and McConaghy, N.: Two clinically discrete syndromes of transsexualism. *Br J Psychiatry*, *133*:73-76, 1978.

Bulliet, C.: *Venus Castine: Famous Female Impersonators Celestial and Human*. New York, Covici, Friede, 1928.

Bullough, V.L.: Transvestites in the Middle Ages: A sociological analysis. *Am J Sociol*, 79:1381-1394. 1974.

Bullough, V.L.: Transsexualism in history. *Arch Sex Behav*, 4(5):561-571, 1975.

Butler, S.R., Suskind, M.R., and Schanberg, S.M.: Maternal behavior as a regulator of polyamine biosynthesis in brain and heart of the developing rat pup. *Science, 199*:445-447, 1978.

Carter, J.N., Tyson, J.E., Tolis, G., Vliet, S.V., Faiman, C.H., and Friesen, H.G.: Prolactin-secreting tumors and hypogonadism in 22 men. *N Engl J Med, 299*:847-852, 1978.

Childs, B., Grumbach, M.M., and Van Wyk, J.J.: Virilizing adrenal hyperplasia, a genetic and hormonal study. *J Clin Invest, 35*:213, 1956.

Christensen v. Thornby, 192 Minn. 123, 255. N.W. 620, 1934.

Ciba-Zeitschrift: Hermaphroditisimus (quoting the *Baseler Chronick*, 1624). *Ciba-Zeitschrift, 5*(57):1920, 1952.

Clarren, S.K. and Smith, D.W.: The fetal alcohol syndrome. *N Engl J Med, 298*:19, 1063-1067, 1978.

Coleman, T.F. and Ganderd, D. (Eds.): Legal section, recent court cases. *J Homosex, 1(3)*:277-293, 1976.

Commonwealth v. Farrell, 322 Mass. 606. 78 N.E.2d 697, 1948.

Cory, D.W.: *The Homosexual in America*, 2nd ed. New York, Castle Pub Co, 1960.

Counseller, V.S. and Sluder, F.J.: Treatment for congenital absence of the vagina. *Surg Clin North Amer, 24*:938. 1944.

Crompton, L.: Homosexuals and the death penalty in colonial America. *J Homosex, 1(3)*:277-293, 1976.

Culliton, B.J.: Scientists dispute book's claim that human clone has been born. *Science, 199*:1314-1316, 1978.

Dahlöf, L.G., Hård, E. and Larsson, K.: Influence of maternal stress on offspring sexual behavior. *Anim Behav, 25*:958-963, 1977.

Darwin, C.R.: *The Origin of Species*. London, John Murray Pub, 1859.

Davidson, J.M.: Neurohormonal bases of male sexual behavior, international review of physiology. In Greep, R.O. (Ed.): *Reproductive Physiology II*, Vol. 13. Baltimore, Univ Park, 1977.

Davidson, P.: Transsexualism in Klinefelter's syndrome. *Psychosomatics,* 7:94, 1966.

Davies, B.M. and Morgenstern, F.S.: A case of cysticercosis, temporal lobe epilepsy, and transvestism. *J Neurol Neurosurg Psychiatry, 23*:247-249, 1960.

Derogatis, L.R., Meyer, J.K., and Vazquez, B.A.: A psychological profile of the transsexual. Part 1: The male. *J Nerv Ment Dis, 166*:234-254, 1978.

De Savitsch, E.: *Homosexuality, Transvestism and Change of Sex*. London, Wm. Heinemann Medical Books, 1958.

Döerr, P., Kockott, G., Vogt, H.J., Pirke, K.M., and Dittmar, F.: Plasma testosterone, estradiol and semen analysis in male homosexuals. *Arch Gen Psychiatry, 29*:829-833, 1973.

Dörner, G., Rohde, W., Seidel, K., Haas, W., and Schott, G.: On the evocability of a positive oestrogen feedback action on LH secretion in transsexual men and women. *Endokrinologie, 67(1)*:20-25, 1976.

Dörner, G., Rohde, W., Stahl, F., Krell, L., and Masius, W.G.: A neuro-endocrine predisposition for homosexuality in men. *Arch Sex Behav, 4(1)*:1-8, 1975.

Durant, W.: *Caesar and Christ.* New York, S&S, 1944.

Edgerton, M.T.: Transsexualism—A surgical problem? (editorial). *Plast Reconstr Surg, 52*:1, 74-77, 1973.

Edgerton, M.T.: The surgical treatment of male transsexuals. *Clin Plast Surg, 1*:2, 285, 1974.

Edgerton, M.T. and Bull, J.: Surgical construction of the vagina and labia in male transsexuals. *Plast Reconstr Surg, 46*:529-539, 1970.

Edgerton, M.T. and Meyer, J.K.: Surgical and psychiatric aspects of trans-sexualism. In Horton, C. (Ed.): *Plastic and Reconstructive Surgery of the Genital Area.* Boston, Little, 1973, pp. 117-161.

Ehrhardt, A.A., Evers, K., and Money, J.: Influence of androgen and some aspects of sexually dimorphic behavior in women with the late-treated adrenogenital syndrome. *Johns Hopkins Med J, 123(3)*:115-122, 1968.

Ellis, A. and Abarbanel, A. (Eds.): *The Encyclopedia of Sexual Behavior,* Vol. 1. New York, Hawthorne, 1961, p. 485.

Emery, A.E.H.: *Elements of Medical Genetics.* Edinburgh, London, Churchill-Livingstone, 1974.

Erickson Educational Foundation Newsletter, 9: No. 1, 1976.

Evans, B.: *Natural History of Nonsense.* New York, Knopf, 1971.

Fenichel, O.: *The Psychoanalytic Theory of Neurosis.* New York, Norton, 1945, pp. 328-341.

Fischelson, L.: Protogynous sex reversal in the fish *Anthias squamipinnis* regulated by the presence or absence of a male fish. *Nature, 227*:90, 1970.

Fisk, N.M.: Gender dysphoria syndrome. *West J Med, 120*:386-391, 1974.

Frank, E., Anderson, C., and Rubinstein, D.: Frequency of sexual dys-function in "normal" couples. *N Engl J Med, 299*:3, 111-115, 1978.

Frantz, A.G.: Prolactin. *N Engl J Med, 298*:4, 201-207, 1978.

Franzini, L.R., Magy, M.A., and Litrownik, A.J.: Detectability and per-ceptions of a transsexual: Implications for therapy. *J Homosex, 2(3)*: 269-279, 1977.

Fratta, W., Biggio, G., and Gessa, G.L.: Homosexual mounting behavior induced in male rats and rabbits by a tryptophan-free diet. *Life Sciences, 21(3)*:379-384 1977.

Freud, S.: Three contributions to the theory of sex; the transformation of puberty (1905). In *The Basic Writings of Sigmund Freud,* trans. A.A. Brill. New York, Random, 1938.

Fryer v. U.S., 207 F.2d 134, 1953.

Gabbe, S.G. and Quilligan, E.J.: Fetal carbohydrate metabolism: Its clinical importance. *Am J Obstet Gynecol*, 127:92-103, 1977.

Gadpaille, W.J.: Research into the physiology of maleness and femaleness: Its contributions to the etiology and psychodynamics of homosexuality. *Arch Gen Psychiatry*, 26:193-206, 1972.

Gawienowski, A.M. and Hodgen, G.D.: Homosexual activity in male rats after p-chlorophenylalanine: Effects of hypophysectomy and testosterone. *Physiol Behav*, 7:551-555, 1971.

The Gazette, Montreal, December 26, 1973, p. 10.

Geis, G., Wright, R., Garrett, T., and Wilson, P.R.: Reported consequences of decriminalization of consensual adult homosexuality in seven American states. *J Homosex*, 1(4):419-426, 1976.

Gerald, P.S.: Sex chromosome disorders. *N Engl J Med*, 294:13, 706-708, 1976.

Gilbert, O.: *Man in Woman's Guise*. London, John Lane Pub, 1926.

Glass, J.D.: Photically evoked potentials from cat neocortex before and after recovery from visual deprivation. *Exp Neurol*, 39:123-139, 1973.

Glass, S.J., Deul, H.J., and Wright, C.A.: Sex hormone studies in male homosexuality. *Endocrinology*, 26:590-594, 1940.

Glaus, A.: Zur Lebensgeschichte eines Transvestiten. *Monatsschr Psychiatr Neurol*, 124:245-258, 1952.

Goldstein, M.: Brain research and violence: Neurochemical, endocrine, pharmacological and genetic studies. *Arch Neurol*, 30:8-23, 1974.

Goodich, M.: Sodomy in ecclesiastical law and theory. *J Homosex*, 1(4): 427-433, 1976.

Goodman. D.J.: The behavior of hypersexual delinquent girls. *Am J Psychiatry*, 133(6):662-668, 1976.

Gordon, G.G., Altman, K., Southren, A.L., Rubin, E., and Lieber, C.S.: Effect of alcohol (ethanol) administration on sex-hormone metabolism in normal men. *N Engl J Med*, 295:15, 793-797, 1976.

Goy, R.W.: Organizing effects of androgen on the behavior of rhesus monkeys. In Michel, R.P. (Ed.): *Endocrinology and Human Behavior*. London, Oxford U P, 1968, pp. 12-31.

Goy, R.W. and Goldfoot, D.A.: Neuroendocrinology: Animal models and problems of human sexuality. In Rubinstein, A.E., Green, R., and Becher, E. (Eds.): *New Directions in Sex Research*. New York, Plenum Pr, 1976, pp. 83-98.

Goy, R.W. and Phoenix, C.H.: The effects of testosterone propionate administered before birth on the development of behavior in genetic female rhesus monkeys. In Sawyer, C. and Gorski, R. (Eds.): *Steroid Hormones and Brain Function*. Berkeley, U of Cal Pr, 1971, pp. 193-201.

Green, R.: Physician emotionalism in the treatment of the transsexual. *Am NY Acad Sci* 29(4):440-443, 1966-67.

Green, R.: Mythological, historical and cross cultural aspects of transsexualism. In Green, R. and Money, J.: *Transsexualism and Sex Reassignment*. Baltimore, Johns Hopkins, 1969, pp. 13-23.

Green, R.: Persons seeking sex change—Psychiatric management of special problems. *Am J Psychiatry, 126*:1596-1603, 1970.

Green, R.: Sexual identity of 37 children raised by homosexual or transsexual parents. *Am J Psychiatry, 135,6*:692-697, 1978.

Green, R. and Money, J. (Eds.): *Transsexualism and Sex Reassignment*. Baltimore, Johns Hopkins, 1969.

Greenough, W.T., Volkmar, F.R., and Juraska, J.M.: Effects of rearing complexity on dendritic branching in frontolateral and temporal cortex of the rat. *Exp Neurol, 41*:371-378, 1973.

Griswold v. Connecticut, 381 U.S. 479, 85 S. Ct. 1678, 14 L. Ed. 2d 510, 1965.

Group for the Advancement of Psychiatry: *Report on Homosexuality with Particular Emphasis on this Problem in Governmental Agencies*. Report No. 30, Topeka, Kansas, 1955.

Grumbach, M.M. and Ducharm, J.R.: The effects of androgens on fetal sexual development. *Fertil Steril, 11*:157, 1960.

Gunnison, F.: The homophile movement in America. In Weltze, R.W. (Ed.): *The Same Sex: An Appraisal of Homosexuality*. Philadelphia, Pilgrim, 1969.

Guze, H.: The transsexual patient: A problem in self-perception. *Ann NY Acad Sci, 29(4)*:464-467, 1966-67.

Haeberle, E.J.: *The Sex Atlas—A New Illustrated Guide*. New York, Seabury, 1978.

Halbreich, U., Segal, S., and Chowers, I.: Day-to-day variations in serum levels of follicle-stimulating hormone and luteinizing hormone in homosexual males. *Biol Psychiatry, 13*:541-550, 1978.

Hamburger, C., Sturrap, G., and Dahl-Iversen, E.: Transvestism. *JAMA, 152*:391-396, 1953.

Hampson, J.G.: Hermaphroditic genital appearance, rearing and eroticism in hyperadrenocorticism. *Bull Johns Hopkins Hosp, 96*:265-273, 1955.

Hansard 814:118: 1827 ff

Hartin v. Director of Bureau of Records, 75 Misc. 2d 229, 347 N.Y.S.2d 515, 1973.

Haworth, J.C. and Dilling, L.A.: Relationships between maternal glucose intolerance and neonatal blood glucose. *J Pediatr, 89*:5, 810-813, 1976.

Henderson, N.D.: Short exposures to enriched environments can increase genetic variability of behavior in mice. *Dev Psychobiol, 9(6)*:549-553, 1976.

Hess, W.R. and Brügger, M.: Das Subcorticale Zentrum der Affektiven Abwehrreaction. *Helv Physiol Pharmacol Acta, 1*:33-52, 1943.

Hierons. R. and Saunders, M.: Impotence in patients with temporal lobe lesions. *Lancet, 2*:761-764, 1966.

Hirsch, H.V.B. and Spinelli, D.N.: Visual experience modifies distribution of horizontally and vertically oriented receptive fields in cats. *Science, 168*:869-871, 1970.

Hoenig, J.: The management of transsexualism. *Can Psychiatr Assoc J, 19*:1-6, 1974.

Hoenig, J.: The legal position of the transsexual: Mostly unsatisfactory outside Sweden. *Can Med Assoc J, 116*:319-323. 1977.

Hoenig, J. and Hamilton, C.: Epilepsy and sexual orgasm. *Acta Psychiatr Neurol Scand, 35*:448-457, 1960.

Hoenig, J., Kenna, J.C., and Youd, A.: Surgical treatment for transsexualism. *Acta Psychiatr Scand, 47*:106-133, 1971.

Hoffman, M.: *The Gay World: Homosexuality and the Social Creation of Evil.* New York, Bantam, 1969.

Holloway, J.P.: *Transsexuals: Their Legal Sex,* 40 U. Col. L. Rev. 283 (1968).

Holloway, J.P.: Transsexuals: Legal considerations. *Arch Sex Behav, 3(1)*:33-50, 1974.

Holmes, L.B.: Genetic counseling for the older pregnant woman: New data and questions. *N Eng J Med, 298*:25, 1419-1421, 1978.

Hooshmand, H. and Brawley, B.: Temporal lobe seizure and exhibitionism. *Neurology, 19*:1119-1124, 1969.

Horrobin, D.F.: *Prolactin,* vol. 5. St. Louis, Eden. 1977.

Hubel, D.H. and Wiesel, T.N.: Receptive fields of single neurones in the cat's striate cortex. *J Physiol, 148*:574-591, 1959.

Hubel, D.H. and Wiesel, T.N.: The period of susceptibility to the physiological effects of unilateral eye closure in kittens. *J Physiol, 206*:419-436, 1970.

Hunter, R., Logue, V., and McMenemy, W.H.: Temporal lobe epilepsy supervening on long-standing transvestism and fetishism. *Epilepsia, 4*:60-65, 1963.

Ionescu, B., Maxmilian, C., and Bucur, A.: Two cases of transsexualism with gonadal dysgenesis. *Br J Psychiatry, 119*:311-314, 1971.

Itil, M.T.: Neurophysiological effects of hormones in humans: Computer EEG profiles of sex and hypothalamic hormones. In Sachar, E.J. (Ed.): *Hormones, Behavior and Psychopathology.* New York, Raven, 1976, pp. 31-40.

James, T.E.: Legal issues of transsexualism in England. In Green, R. and Money, J. (Eds.): *Transsexualism and Sex Reassignment.* Baltimore, Johns Hopkins, 1969.

Jessin v. County of Shasta, 274 C.A.2d 737, 79 C.R. 359, 1969.

Johnson, H.D. and Vanjonack, W.J.: Symposium: Stress and health of the dairy cow. *J of Dairy Science, 59(9)*:1603-1617, 1976.

Jones, H., Schirmer, H., and Hoopes, J.: A sex conversion operation for males with transsexualism. *Am J Obstet Gynecol. 100*:101, 1968.

Jost, A.: Problems of fetal endocrinology: The gonadal and hypophyseal hormones. *Recent Prog Horm Res, 8*:302, 1959.

Kaada, B.R.: Stimulation and regional ablation of the amygdaloid complex with reference to functional representation. In Eleftheriou, B.E. (Ed.): *The Neurobiology of the Amygdala.* New York, Plenum, 1972.

Kalhan, S.C., Savin, S.M., and Adam, P.A.J.: Attenuated glucose production rate in newborn infants of insulin-dependent diabetic mothers. *N Engl J Med, 296*:375-376, 1977.

Kandel, E.: *Cellular Basis of Behavior.* San Francisco, Freeman, 1976.

Kinsey, A.C.: *Sexual Behavior in the Human Male.* Philadelphia, Saunders, 1948.

Kinsey, A.C.: *Sexual Behavior in the Human Female.* Philadelphia, Saunders, 1953.

Klotz, H.P., Borel, E., and Colla, R.: Le travestissement hétérosexual habituel. Forme particulière des ambiguités sexuelles constitutionnelles. *Sem Hop Paris, 65*:3438, 1955.

Knorr, N.J.: The transsexual's request for surgery. *J Nerv Ment Dis, 147*:517-524, 1968.

Kockott, G. and Nusselt, L.: Zur Frage der cerebralen Dysfunktion bei der Transsexualität. *Nervenarzt, 47*:310-318, 1976.

Kolata, G.B.: Behavioral development: Effects of environments. *Science, 189*:207-209, 1975.

Kolodny, R.C., Jacobs, L.S., and Daughaday, W.H.: Mammary stimulation causes prolactin secretion in nonlactating women. *Nature, 238*:284-286, 1972.

Kolodny, R.C., Jacobs, L.S., Masters, W.H., Toro, G., and Daughaday, W.H.: Plasma gonadotrophins and prolactin in male homosexuals. *Lancet, II(7766)*:18-20, 1972.

Kolodny, R.C., Masters, W.H., Hendryx, J., and Toro, G.: Plasma testosterone and semen analysis in male homosexuals. *N Engl J Med, 285*:1170-1174, 1971.

Koranyi, E.K.: Sex change surgery in a male transsexual. *Psychiatr J U Ottawa, 1(3)*:113-122, 1976.

Koranyi, E.K.: Medical considerations at intake. *Poca Press, 12(1)*:May, 1978.

Koranyi, E.K.: *Reflections on Modern Sex Therapies.* Presented at International College of Psychosomatic Medicine Sixth Annual Psychosomatic Seminar, Plattsburgh, New York, September 22-23, 1978.

Koranyi, E.K.: Morbidity and rate of undiagnosed physical illnesses in a psychiatric clinic population. *Arch Gen Psychiatry, 36*:414-419, 1979.

Krause, W.: Influence of DDT, DDVP and malathion on FSH, LH and testosterone serum levels and testosterone concentration in testis. *Bull Environ Contam Toxicol, 18(2)*:231-242, 1977.

Kupperman, H.S.: The endocrine status of the transsexual patient. *Ann NY Acad Sci, 29(4)*:434-439, 1966-67.

Lamarck, J.B.: *Systéme des Animaux sans Vertèbres,* 1801.

Langevin, R., Paitich, D., and Steiner, B.: The clinical profile of male transsexuals living as females vs. those living as males. *Arch Sex Behav,* 6(2):143-154, 1977.

Laub, D. and Fisk, W.: A rehabilitation program for gender dysphoria syndrome by surgical sex change. *Plast Reconstr Surg,* 53:388-403, 1974.

In re Leber, Neuchâtel Cantonal Court, July 2, 1945.

Lebovitz, P.S.: Feminine behavior in boys: Aspects of its outcome. *Am J Psychiatry, 128(10):*1283-1289, 1972.

Lenton, E.A., Milner, G.R., Cooke, I.D., Jenner, F.A., and Sampson, G.A.: Episodic secretion of growth hormone in a male trans-sexual during treatment with oestrogen both before and after orchidectomy. *J Endocrinol,* 74:337-338, 1977.

Levine, E.M., Gruenewald, D., and Shaiova, C.H.: Behavioral differences and emotional conflict among male-to-female transsexuals. *Arch Sex Behav, 5(1):*81-86, 1976.

Levine, S.B. and Yost, M.A., Jr.: Frequency of sexual dysfunction in a general gynecological clinic: An epidemiological approach. *Arch Sex Behav, 5(3):*229-238, 1976.

In re Lifschutz, 2 C.3d 415, 467 P.2d 557, 85 C.R. 829, 1970.

Lipshultz, L.I. and Corriere, M., Jr.: Construction of a neo-vagina in the male transsexual. In *Proceedings, Symposium on the Human Vagina in Health Disease.* Detroit, Michigan, Wayne State University, Oct. 28-30, 1976, p. 31.

Lönnerdal, B., Forsum, E., Gebre-Medhin, M. and Hambraeus, L.: Breast milk composition in Ethiopian and Swedish mothers. II. Lactose, nitrogen and protein contents 1-3. *Am J Clin Nutr,* 29:1134-1141, 1976.

Loraine, J.A., Ismail, A.A.A., Adamopoulos, D.A., and Dove, G.A.: Endocrine function in male and female homosexuals. *Br Med J,* 4:406-408, 1970.

Lorenz, K.Z.: *On Aggression,* trans. Latzke. London, Methuen & Co., Ltd., 1967.

Lothstein, L.M.: The psychological management and treatment of hospitalized transsexuals. *J Nerv Ment Dis, 166:*255-262, 1978.

Lowy, F.H. and Kolivakis, T.: Autocastration in a male transsexual. *Can Psychiatr Assoc J, 16(5):*399, 1971.

Lund, J.S. and Lund, R.D.: The effects of varying periods of visual deprivation on synaptogenesis in the superior colliculus of the rat. *Brain Res,* 42:21-32, 1972.

Lundberg, P.O., Sjövall, A., and Wålinder, J.: Sella turcica in male-to-female transsexuals. *Arch Sex Behav, 4(6):*657-662, 1975.

Lyon, M.F.: Gene action in the mammalian X chromosome of the mouse (*Mus musculus* L.). *Nature, 190:*372, 1961.

MacLean, P.D.: The limbic system ("visceral brain") and emotional be-havior. *Arch Neurol Psychiatr, 73*:130-134, 1955.

MacLean, P.D.: The triune brain, emotion and scientific bias. In Schmitt, F.O. (Ed.): *The Neurosciences: Second Study Program.* New York, Rockefeller, 1970.

Mandel, A.J. and Geyer, M.A.: Hallucinations: Chemical and physiological. In Grenell, R.G. and Gabay, S. (Eds.): *Biological Foundations of Psychiatry*, vol. 2. New York, Raven, 1976, pp. 729-754.

Margolese, M.S. and Janiger, O.: Androsterone/etiocholanolone ratios in male homosexuals. *Br Med J, 3*:207-210, 1973.

Markland, C.: Transsexual surgery. *Obstet Gynecol Ann, 4*:309-330, 1975.

Maslow, A.H.: *The Psychology of Science: A Reconnaisance.* New York, Har-Row, 1966.

Mata, L.J., Urutia, J.J., and Lechtig, A.: Infection and nutrition of children of a low socioeconomic rural community. *Am J Clin Nutr, 24*:249, 1971.

McIndoe, A.: Treatment of congenital absence and obliterative conditions of the vagina. *Br J Plast Surg, 2*:254, 1950.

McKee, E.A., Roback, H.B., and Hollender, M.H.: Transsexualism in two male triplets. *Am J Psychiatry, 133(3)*:334-337, 1976.

McKinney, W.T., Jr., Suomi, S.J., and Harlow, H.F.: Experimental psycho-pathology in nonhuman primates. In Arieti, S. (Ed.): *American Hand-book of Psychiatry*, 2nd ed., vol. 6. New York, Basic, 1975, pp. 310-334.

Mehl, M.: Transsexualism: A perspective. In Laub, D. and Gondy, P. (Eds.): *Proceedings of the Second Interdisciplinary Symposium on Gender Dysphoria Syndrome.* Stanford, California, Stanford University Medical Center, 1973, pp. 15-19.

Mennuti, M.T.: Prenatal genetic diagnosis: Current status. *N Engl J Med, 297(18)*:1004-1006, 1977.

Meyer-Bahlburg, H.F.L.: Prenatal effects of sex hormones on human male behavior: Medroxyprogesterone acetate (MPA). *Psychoneuroendo-crinology, 2*:383-390, 1977.

Meyer-Bahlburg, H.F.L.: Sex hormones and male homosexuality in com-parative perspectives. *Arch Sex Behav, 6(4)*:297-325, 1977.

Meyerson, B.J. and Lindstrom, L.: Sexual motivation in the neonatally androgenized female rat. *Horm Brain Function* (Budapest), 443-448, 1973.

Mitchell, W., Falconer, M.A., and Hill, D.: Epilepsy with fetishism relieved by temporal lobectomy. *Lancet 2*:626-630, 1954.

Money, J.: Hermaphroditism, gender and precocity in hyperadrenocorti-cism. *Bull Johns Hopkins Hosp, 96*:253-264, 1955.

Money, J.: Cytogenetic and other aspects of transvestism and transsexualism. *J Sex Res, 3*:141-143, 1967.

Money, J.: In Green, R. and Money, J. (Eds.): *Transsexualism and Sex Reassignment*. Baltimore, Johns Hopkins, 1969.

Money, J. and Dalery, J.: Iatrogenic homosexuality: Gender identity in seven 46XX chromosomal females with hyperadrenocortical hemaphroditism born with a penis, three reared as boys, four reared as girls. *J Homosex, 1*(4):357-371, 1976.

Money, J. and Caskin, R.: Sex reassignment. *Int J Psychiatry, 0*:240-260, 1970-71.

Money, J., Hampson, J.G., and Hampson, J.L.: An examination of basic sexual concept: The evidence of human hermaphroditism. *Bull Johns Hopkins Hosp*, 97:301-319, 1955.

Money, J., Hampson, J.G., and Hampson, J.L.: Imprinting and the establishment of gender role. *AMA Arch Neurol Psychiatry*, 77:333-336, 1957.

Money, J. and Lewis, V.: IQ, genetics and accelerated growth: Adrenogenital syndrome. *Bull Johns Hopkins Hosp, 118*:365, 1966.

Money, J. and Schwartz, F.: Public opinion and social issues in transsexualism: A case study in medical sociology. In Green, R. and Money, J. (Eds.): *Transsexualism and Sex Reassignment*. Baltimore, Johns Hopkins, 1969.

Money, J. and Wolff, G.: Sex reassignment: Male to female to male. *Arch Sex Behav, 2*(3):245-250, 1973.

Morin, L.P.: Progesterone: Inhibition of rodent sexual behavior. *Physiol Behav, 18*:701-715, 1977.

MT v. JT, 355 A.2d 204 (Sup. Ct. App. Div. N.J. 1976).

Nelson, C., Paitch, D., and Steiner, B.W.: Medicolegal aspects of transsexualism. *Can Psychiatr Assoc J, 21*:557-564, 1976.

Nelson, R., Lützow, A.V., Kolb, H., and Gouras, P.: Horizontal cells in cat retina with independent dendritic systems. *Science, 189*:137-139, 1975.

Nestlerode v. U.S., 122 F.2d 56, 1941.

New York Times, March 12, 1978.

Newman, L.E. and Stoller, R.J.: Nontranssexual men who seek sex reassignment. *Am J Psychiatry, 131*(4):437-441, 1974.

Nusselt, L. and Kockott, G.: EEG-Befunde bei Transsexualität—ein Beitrag zur Pathogenese. *Z EEG EMG*, 7:42-48, 1976.

Ohno, S.: Sexual differentiation and testosterone production. *N Engl J Med*, 295(18):1011-1012, 1976.

Olds, J. and Milner, P.: Positive reinforcement produced by electrical stimulation of septal area and other regions of rat brain. *J Comp Physiol Psychol*, 47:419-427, 1954.

Ormrod, R.: The medico-legal aspects of sex determination. *Med Leg J, 40*(3):78-88, 1972.

Papez, J.W.: A proposed mechanism of emotions. *Arch Neurol Psychiatr,* 38:725-743, 1937.

Parks, G.A., Korth-Schütz, S., Penny, R., Hilding, R.F., Dumars, K.W., Frasier, D., and New, M.I.: Variations in pituitary-gonadal function in adolescent male homosexuals and heterosexuals. *J Clin Endocrinol Metab,* 39:796-801, 1974.

Pauly, I.B.: Male psychosexual inversion: Transsexualism. A review of 100 cases. *Arch Gen Psychiatry,* 13:172, 1965.

Pauly, I.B.: The current status of the change of sex operation. *J Nerv Ment Dis,* 147:460-471, 1968.

People *ex rel* Burke v. Steinberg, 190 Misc. 413, 73 N.Y.S.2d 475, 1947.

People v. Samuels, 250 C.A.2d 501, 58 C.R. 439, 1967.

Person, E. and Ovesey, L.: The transsexual syndrome in males. *Am J Psychother,* 28(1):1974.

Pettigrew, J.D.: The importance of early visual experience for neurons of the developing geniculostriate system. *Invest Ophthalmol,* 11:386-394, 1972.

Phoenix, C.H., Goy, R.W., Gerall, A.A., and Young, W.C.: Organizing action of prenatally administered testosterone propionate on the tissues mediating mating behavior in the female guinea pig. *Endocrinology,* 65:369-382, 1959.

Ploeger, A. and Flamm, R.: Synopsis des Transvestismus und Transsexualismus. *Fortschr Neurol Psychiatr,* 44(9):493-555, 1976.

Polani, P.E.: Hormonal and clinical aspects of hermaphroditism and the testicular feminizing syndrome in man. *Philos Trans R Soc Lond,* Series B, 259:187, 1970.

Presser, C.S.: Legal problems attendant to sex reassignment surgery. *J Leg Med,* 5:17-24, 1977.

Radcliffe Report: Security Procedures in the Public Service. London, H.M.S.D., 1962.

Randell, J.: Pre-operative and post-operative status of male and female transsexuals. In Green, R. and Money, J. (Eds.): *Transsexualism and Sex Reassignment.* Baltimore, Johns Hopkins, 1969, pp. 355-381.

Randall (formerly Christian) v. Christian (No. 32964), (Int. Jud. Ct. Nov. 1973).

Reinisch, J.M.: Effects of prenatal hormone exposure on physical and psychological development in humans and animals with a note on the state of the field. In Sachar, E.J. (Ed.): *Hormones, Behavior and Psychopathology.* New York, Raven, 1976, pp. 69-94.

Reitano, J.F., Caminos-Torres, R., and Snyder, P.J.: Serum LH and FSH responses to repetative administration of gonadotropin-releasing hormone in patients with idiopathic hypogonadic hypogonadism. *J Clin Endocrinol Metab.* 41:1035-1042, 1975.

Roback, H., McKee, E., Vogelfanger, R., and Corney, R.: Gender identification and the female impersonator. *South Med J, 68(4)*:459-462, 1975.

Roe v. Wade, 410 U.S. 113, 35 L.Ed.2d 147, 93 S. Ct. 705, 1973.

Rorvick, D.: *In His Image, The Cloning of a Man.* Philadelphia, Lippincott, 1978.

Routier, S., Paget, M., Ernst, J.. Langerson, P., Wiart, P., Duthoit, F., and Cousin, J.: Tumeur feminisante de la surrénale et transsexualisme. *Ann Endocrinol, 25*:680, 1964.

Sachar, E.J. (Ed.): *Hormones, Behavior and Psychopathology.* New York, Raven, 1976.

Sachs, B.D., Pollak, E.I., Schoelch-Kreiger, M., and Barfield, R.J.: Sexual behavior: Normal male patterning in androgenized female rats. *Science, 181*:770-772, 1973.

Sagarin, E. and MacNamara, D.E.J.: The homosexual as a crime victim. *International Journal of Criminology and Penology, 3*:14-25, 1975.

Sandler, M. and Gessa, G.L.: *Sexual Behavior—Pharmacology and Biochemistry.* New York, Raven, 1975.

Sayadoff v. Warda, 125 C.A.2d 626, 270 P.2d 140, 1954.

Schapiro, S. and Vukovich, K.R.: Early experience effects upon cortical dendrites: A proposed model for development. *Science, 167*:292-294, 1970.

Selby, L.A., Menges, R.W., Houser, E.C., Flatt, R.E., and Chase, A.C.: Outbreak of swine malformations associated with wild black cherry, *Prunus serotina. Arch Environ Health, 22*:496, 1971.

Sharma, R.P.: Light-dependent homosexual activity in males of a mutant of *Drosophila melanogaster. Experientia, 33(2)*:171-173, 1977.

Sherwin, R.: Legal aspects of male transsexualism. In Green, R. and Money, J. (Eds.): *Transsexualism and Sex Reassignment.* Baltimore, Johns Hopkins, 1969.

Simpson, J.L.: *Disorders of Sexual Differentiation: Etiology and Clinical Delineation.* New York, Acad Pr, 1976.

Slovenko, R.: *Psychiatry and Law.* Boston, Little, 1973.

Smith, D.: *Transsexualism, Sex Reassignment Surgery and the Law.* 56 CORNELL L. REV. 963 (1971).

Socarides, C.E.: A psychoanalytic study of the desire for sexual transformation ("transsexualism"): The plaster-of-Paris man. *Int J Psychoanal, 51*:341-349, 1970.

Soulairac, A. and Soulairac, M.L.: Relationships between the nervous and endocrine regulation of sexual behavior in male rats. *Psychoneuroendocrinology, 3*:17-29, 1978.

Spitz, R.A.: The psychogenic diseases in infancy. In *The Psychoanalytic Study of the Child,* vol. 6. New York, Int Univ Pr, 1951, p. 255.

Stahl, F., Dörner, G., Ahrens, L., and Graudenz, W.: Significant decreased apparently free testosterone levels in plasma of male homosexuals. *Endocrinologie, 68*:115-117, 1976.

State v. Fransua, 85 N.M. 173, 510 P.2d 106, 1973.

State v. Roby, 83 Vt. 121, 74 A. 638, 1909.

Staughton, G. et al.: *Charter of William Penn and Laws of the Commonwealth of Pennsylvania.* Harrisburg, Lane S. Hart, 1879.

Stoller, R.J.: A contribution to the study of gender identity. *Int J Psychoanal, 45*:220-226, 1964.

Stoller, R.J.: Etiological factors in male transsexualism. *Ann NY Acad Sci,* 29(4), 1966-67.

Stoller, R.J.: Male childhood transsexualism. *J Am Acad Child Psychiatry,* 7(2):193-209, 1968.

Stoller, R.J.: A biased view of sex transformation operation. *J Nerv Ment Dis, 149*:312-317, 1969.

Stoller, R.J.: Male transsexualism: Uneasiness. *Am J Psychiatry, 130*(5): 536-539, 1973.

Stoller, R.J.: Psychoanalytic diagnosis. Definition and classification of cross dressing. In Rakoff, V.M., Stancer, H.C., and Kedward, H.B (Eds.): *Psychiatric Diagnosis.* New York, Brunner-Mazel, 1977.

Stoller, R.J., Garfinkel, H., and Rosen, A.: Passing and maintenance of sexual identification in intersexual patients. *Arch Gen Psychiatry,* 2:379, 1960.

Stone, C.B.: Psychiatric screening for transsexual surgery. *Psychosomatics, XVIII*:25-27, 1977.

Sussman, N.: Sex and sexuality in history. In Saddock, B.J., Kaplan, H.I., and Freedman, A.M. (Eds.): *The Sexual Experience.* Baltimore, Williams & Wilkins, 1976, pp. 7-70.

Uhlenbruck, W.: Transsexualatät und personalitaten. *Med Klin, 64*:1178, 1969.

U.S. v. Cook, 462 F.2d 301, 303, 1972.

U.S. v. Vollweiler, 229 F.S. 558, 1964.

Van Putten, T. and Fawzy, F.I.: Sex conversion surgery in a man with severe gender dysphoria. *Arch Gen Psychiatry, 33*:751-753, 1976.

Voyler v. Ralph K. Davies Medical Center, 403 F.S. 456, 1975.

Wachtel, S.S., Ohno, S., and Koo, G.C.: Possible role of H-Y antigen in the primary determination of sex. *Nature, 257*:235-236, 1975.

Wålinder, J.: Transsexualism: Definition, prevalence and sex distribution. *Acta Psychiatr Scand [Suppl], 203*:255-258, 1967.

Walton, T.: Transsexualism: When is a woman not a woman? *New Law Journal,* May, 1974.

West, D.J.: *Homosexuality.* Harmondsworth, Middlesex, England, Pelican Books, Ltd., 1968.

Wetherbee, M. and Coleman, T.F. (Eds.): Recent court cases. *J Homosex,* 2(2):173-182, Winter 1976-77.

Wilkins, L., Jones, H.W., Jr., Holdman, G.H., and Stempfel, R.S.: Masculinization of the female fetus associated with administration of oral and intramuscular progestins during gestation: Non-adrenal female pseudohermaphroditism. *J Clin Endocrinol Metab, 18*:559, 1958.

Wilson, J.G. and Warkany, J.: Malformations in the genito-urinary tract induced by maternal vitamin A deficiency in the rat. *Am J Anat, 83:* 357, 1948.

Wilson, P.R. and Chappell, D.: Australian attitudes towards abortion, prostitution and homosexuality. *Australian Quarterly, 40:*7-17, 1968.

Yalom, I.D., Green, R., and Fisk, N.: Prenatal exposure to female hormones. *Arch Gen Psychiatry, 28:*554-561, 1973.

Yamamoto, T.: Sex differentiation. In Moar, W.S. and Randall, D.J. (Eds.): *Fish Physiology.* New York, Acad Pr, 1969.

Yardley, K.M.: Training in feminine skills in a male transsexual: A pre-operative procedure. *Br J Med Psychol, 49:*329-339, 1976.

INDEX